And Baby Makes Four

And Baby Makes Four

*

Karen L. Nutt

Northwest Publishing, Inc.
Salt Lake City, Utah

And Baby Makes Four

For information address: Northwest Publishing, Inc.
6906 South 300 West, Salt Lake City, Utah 84047
JAC 5.1.94
Edited by: Ann Cude

PRINTING HISTORY
First Printing 1994

ISBN: 1-56901-278-4

NPI books are published by Northwest Publishing, Incorporated,
6906 South 300 West, Salt Lake City, Utah 84047.
The name "NPI" and the "NPI" logo are trademarks belonging to
Northwest Publishing, Incorporated.

PRINTED IN THE UNITED STATES OF AMERICA.
10 9 8 7 6 5 4 3 2 1

To my husband, Bryan, for his expertise at reading a home pregnancy test. And special thanks to my daughter, Courtney, who patiently watched *Barney* videos while I wrote this book; to my father-in-law, Frank, for his support, although he'd never admit that I beat him by a stroke after nine holes when I was more than seven months along; and to Baby Nutt, who made four.

First Month

DAY 1

Yesterday I discovered baby makes four.

At approximately 5:27:24 P.M. (EDT) yesterday, an extremely faint dot appeared on my home pregnancy test. And if it weren't for my husband (I'll call him Bryan because that's his name), I wouldn't be pregnant right now. That is, Bryan actually *read* the test's instruction manual to compare my results. I simply *believed* my dot wasn't purple enough, or even pink enough, to signify pregnancy. And I don't have to be a doctor to know that either…I'm a journalist. Anyway, Bryan, who is an engineer—*not* a doctor—insisted that *any* dot means pregnancy. And he kept insisting this until well past 8:41:53 P.M., same time zone, at which time I gave in because I got tired of arguing about it.

I regret that I didn't keep a daily account of my first pregnancy. That way, I would've known that from the 33rd day of gestation (fancy pregnancy term) through the 86th day, I am *supposed* to experience morning bouts of seemingly never-ending stomach aches, complicated by occasional periods of heaving and throwing up.

On the other hand, maybe it's better that I don't know when to throw up.

Without precise recollection of my first pregnancy, I can be spontaneous, creating a one-of-a-kind, special experience that I will never forget.

Especially if I write it all down.

DAY 2

Today marks the second full day of my knowing that I'm pregnant for a second time.

I received a congratulatory call from my OB/GYN after he heard of the results of my *official* pregnancy test. Not that I was *unofficially* pregnant; I just wanted a clinical test to confirm my home pregnancy test.

You know, a second opinion.

Now I'm wondering why I really forked over the $9.94 (on sale) for the home pregnancy test in the first place. I used one about five months ago when "Fred" was tardy. (I'll call it Fred because I've never understood why it's called a period.) I don't recall how much it cost, but I do remember getting a $1.50 refund in the mail. So I did make money on the deal. Anyway, back to the test itself. It was negative, which was fine with me.

Then I found out from my doctor's nurse that home tests could produce a false negative. So she told me, "Now Mrs. Nutt, wait and see if your period starts within a week. If not, you'll need to come to the clinic for a blood test to see if you're pregnant."

So, aside from the buck-fifty, the home test was totally worthless—at least as far as giving me peace of mind. As it turned out, Fred showed up three days later, and that was about as proof positive as I was going to get—and *that* didn't cost me a penny.

Once again, I fell into the "home pregnancy test" trap two days ago. Although it was positive, I still had to go to the clinic for a blood test. Had it been negative, I would have been instructed where to tune in for news and official information in the event of an emergency. In other words, I would have been told to sit and wait for Fred. If and when Fred failed to appear, I would have been told to go to the clinic. Do not pass Go. Do not collect $200.

And that $200 sure would come in handy to pay for all these tests.

DAY 3

Not too many people know yet. It's kind of nice to keep the secret just that—a secret. But Bryan's busting at the seams—not a pretty sight.

Actually, I think it would be fun not to tell anyone else. And as I gradually started to bust at the seams, I'd let people wonder. Then again, I reflect on my first pregnancy—around the fourth month—when I just started wearing maternity clothes. That's the time that if people knew I was pregnant, then I looked pregnant. But if people didn't know, then I looked *fat*. So, I became extremely self-conscious when Bryan and I went to all-you-can-eat buffets. Restaurant owners began to eye me up, down, and mainly in the middle to determine if I were a financial risk to their business.

But all I needed to do was lift my over-sized sweatshirt (we always dine casually) to reveal my elastic waistband (the red badge of pregnancy), and immediately women all around knew that no woman in her right fashion mind would wear elastic on purpose—unless she were pregnant.

That reminds me. It's a good thing I kept my maternity underwear. Those polyester grannies aren't exactly the last word in style, but they certainly do the trick on two specific occasions:

1) When I bust at the seams;

2) When I frankly don't *care* what comes between me and my Calvin Klein's.

You can buy frilly undies specially geared for the woman-with-child. I think they're silly, though, because I don't care how much I glow, a maternity teddy won't make me feel sexy. Just shiny. Maybe Demi Moore baring all on the cover of that skinny-woman's magazine as she busted at the seams can get away with it. If I did that at eight months, the world would laugh at my elastic indentions encircling my stretchmark-ridden tummy. Not a pretty sight.

In fact, remember how some conservative stores wrapped Demi's tummy with brown paper? Was it sexy or did store owners think customers would get grossed out and not impulsively buy that Snickers bar they were going to buy had they not seen all that bulge? Fifty-two cents (including tax) was at stake here. (By the way, that was Demi's *second* pregnancy.)

With me, the brown paper would be an enhancement. Sure beats all that elastic.

DAY 4

I worked out at the gym for the first time since learning of my pregnancy. It's important to stay in shape as your shape begins to change shape.

What's distressing is that it's taken two years since the birth of my firstborn to get back to where I was two years and nine months ago. And I weigh even a few pounds less now than I did then. At Courtney's birth, I topped out at thirty-six pounds of weight gain.

Courtney wasn't a thirty-six-pound baby.

So I left the hospital only nineteen pounds lighter. About seven of those pounds melted off somehow within a few weeks. But the remaining ten were quite stubborn. With my slow-as-molasses metabolism, it took every bit of dieting and exercising I could muster. So I stopped eating molasses. I was just too used to absorbing all those extra calories you get to absorb when you're pregnant—and that's the only time in your life you have license to do so. Eventually, the weight came off, and in recent months I've managed to lose even more.

Now it's time to gain again. From what I've heard, women show earlier with their second pregnancy. Uh-oh. Something about stretched muscles. That I do understand. My stomach has never been the same—not that the "same" was something every model on the cover of *Vogue* or that skinny lady on the Special K cereal commercials should strive for.

Back to the workout. It was brief: fifteen minutes on the Stairmaster, five on the Lifecycle, ten on the basketball court, and fifteen on the track (walking briskly). I used to run, but a back ailment sidelined me from that activity. I play USTA tennis (singles), so I can continue that, and in two months I'll play co-ed softball. The rules for the first pregnancy apply also to the second: don't take up a new sport or strenuous activity you weren't doing before becoming pregnant.

I imagine it will be tough for me to keep it up as my weight inevitably goes up. That was true the first time around. The difference with the second is that I worked so hard after the first to get back into shape. An appropriate analogy here is— and I often ask myself this—Why vacuum the carpet? It's just going to get dirty again. Or why mop the floor? Why wash the clothes? Why do the windows?

Unfortunately, these are activities I was doing *before* becoming pregnant.

DAY 5

Already I'm learning there are some brand-new, tender moments to experience with a second pregnancy. That is, the sharing of the second pregnancy with the product of the first.

I'm not saying this because I'm her mother, but my daughter, Courtney, is probably the smartest child on the face of this earth. Just a smidgen over two, Courtney knows all sorts of things and is a wide conversationalist. That's why she gets invited to lots of parties. An example of her intelligence: ask her who the president is, and she'll promptly reply with a nonpartisan "Buuuuuussssshh!" She enjoys talking about current events. Turn the topic of discussion to landscaping and ask her what that short, stubby green plant is in front of the house and she'll say without hesitation, "buuuuuusssssshh!"

Sure, she has a better concept of the stubby bush than the Bush that's a bit taller. I know a lot of adults who say the same thing. Like a parrot, she can recite many interesting tidbits whose meaning she may not know. She's so cute saying them.

But the most precious is when Bryan or I ask her, "What are you going to be?" Her answer? A doctor? An engineer? Nope.

"A big sister."

DAY 6

Today I have a fever, a sore throat, and achy muscles. Moms aren't allowed to get sick, much less complain that they are sick. That leaves dad with the kid(s). Take off those parentheses, and mom *really* can't get sick. Watching one child is difficult enough for the male species.

I'm lucky. Bryan helps out when he can. It's just that he underestimates himself when it comes to child care. So it's really up to the moms of this world to teach the dads how to fill in during a pinch.

A pinch hitter might be a good way to describe it in terms men can understand. Sexist? Perhaps. Explain to them it's the bottom of the ninth. You're the home team, by the way. With a strong batting average in clutch situations, dad has what it takes to drive home the winning run. If he only does well enough to tie the score, sending the game into extra innings, then he has to hit the mound as relief pitcher. So he'd better get the job done right the first time.

In the meantime, while dad is enjoying this baseball metaphor situation, mom needs to lie down and pamper herself *before* there's a new one in the family that'll need plenty of Pampers.

DAY 7

Feeling a little better today. My throat's still a bit sore, but that's about it.

But to continue this line of complaining, I do have mid-morning sickness. It runs from 10 A.M. until the first commercial break during *Oprah*.

Being sick has reminded me of many common things I must now avoid because I'm pregnant. Aspirin, for example. The only Tylenol I had in the house was Courtney's fruit-flavored drops, so I suffered in silence. Well, not exactly. I did complain and that made me feel somewhat better.

Let's see, other things I must remember to avoid:
• Cats
• Perms
• Cats with perms

Actually, the thing with cats, if I understand it correctly, is that pregnant women should avoid cat (excuse me while I get technical here) excrement in litter boxes. Honestly, I think it's a good idea to avoid cat excrement whether you're pregnant or not.

DAY 8

I apologize for getting a bit gross with the cat stuff yesterday.

Anyway, mid-morning sickness extended well past the mid-morning hours today. Call it dusk sickness. I tried describing it to Bryan: it's like you're really really hungry, so hungry the thought of food makes you queasy. He understood and replied by saying he feels that way, too.

Empathy pains strike again.

But I think he got over his—he had chili for supper while I dined on peanut butter 'n crackers.

During this mid-morning-to-dusk sickness, I played a USTA singles match. As a precaution, I told my captain I was plagued with queasiness for reasons she knew about in case I lost. I didn't lose, by the way. I'm not saying I need a built-in excuse—because throwing up at the time was high on my priority list—but it's good to know I can win in spite of early pregnancy.

DAY 9

February 2. That's the due date handed down by my OB/GYN today.

All this reminds me of salutations. Every person who approaches you at the OB/GYN office doesn't extend normal greetings, such as "Hi. How are you?"

I say, "Hi, my name is Karen—"

And they interrupt with, "When was the first day of your last period?"

A bit personal, I might add. It's also not the sort of thing I keep in my head for ready recollection. Like the cost of Walker 3-size Pampers at Wal-Mart with a dollar-off coupon, including state and federal sales tax ($8.93). But my experience with my first pregnancy taught me to keep that figure in my mind for ready recollection—in case it appeared in a *Jeopardy!* category.

Anyway, it's April 27. It's from that date the doc comes up with a due date, based on typical four-week periods. And he says—and at this point I blush—that conception occurred four or five weeks ago. I have no idea when conception occurred. He sure wasn't there, so how would he know?

He's a doctor.

I guess I'm just a bit disappointed with myself for not knowing because this time around I vowed I would know when I conceived by keeping concise, accurate records of when Bryan and I, well, you know, did what the doctor said we did. My method? I simply use an exclamation point (!) on the dates that conception could've occurred, if you know what I mean. I thought an exclamation point was appropriate—and other normal, healthy, red-blooded American women of two-year-olds probably think so, too.

What happened was that this particular month I was instructed not to get pregnant because of my back ailment, and I was undergoing physical therapy and taking medication for it. So I didn't keep track of those intimate moments on my kitchen calendar because we were being careful.

At least I *thought* we were.

What gets me is that we have friends who know the time, the place and who was on *Letterman* at the time of their child's conception. Take Garth Brooks. No, he's not one of our friends. But he announces to the world their unborn daughter (at this writing) will be named Taylor Mayne. The Mayne is for the state where she was conceived. (Somebody get Garth a dictionary.) And Taylor is for James Taylor. (I don't know how he fits into the conception picture here.)

While I'm happy for the Brookses, I can't even nail down the state where our child's conception took place. But if I did, I'd certainly give the kid a break and spell it correctly.

DAY 10

After finding out the due date, I did what 97.4 percent (1976 figures) of mothers-to-be-again do: research the date for significant historical events.

February 2 is an important day. It's Groundhog Day.

Extensive research of this date reveals many interesting historical notes.

Take, for example, Otto II—not Sarge's dog in "Beetle Bailey"—but of course, I'm talking about the King of the Lombards, who was crowned Holy Roman Emperor on this date in 926 A.D. (I admit I don't know what day Sarge's dog was born.)

Back to Otto II. That makes Otto Nutt. Naw, sounds like a gizmo that connects important stuff in a car engine.

On February 2 in 1534, the Swabian League expired. Probably has to do with the high cost of Q-Tips.

Here's a historical birthdate: Nell Gwyn, actress and mistress of King Charles II of England, was born February 2, 1651. First of all, we can't name her after a mistress—that's kind of tacky. Besides, Nell Nutt is a make-fun-of-and-get-beat-up-on-the-playground name. Other big-name birthdays that came a bit later: James Joyce, Farrah Fawcett, and Tom Smothers.

On this date in 1970, there was a Buffalo Dance at San Filipe Pueblo, New Mexico. Wasn't that where the *Flying Nun's* convent was? And there was a Carrot Carnival in Holtville, California, the following year that began on February 2nd.

But only a small percent of babies are born on their due dates. However, on February 2, 1993, if Baby Nutt II does indeed enter this world *and* see his/her shadow, does that mean we'll have six more weeks of winter?

DAY 11

As I alluded to yesterday, it takes a lot of thought and effort to name our baby. It's not an easy task for parents, but with a last name like Nutt, it's a more tedious process.

Automatically, some names are eliminated right off the bat. Like Hazel. Hickory. Beech. Concerning middle names, it definitely can't begin with a *P*, i.e., John P. Nutt. One syllable first names don't always go well with Nutt. Of course, not many two or three syllable words do, either. And we have to be careful not to get too classy with names. For example, Bryan's middle name is McMillan, and we'd like to keep that if it's a boy. Attach a formal first name, such as Andrew, and you have Andrew McMillan...Nutt. I just don't know.

Perhaps it's more difficult, too, to name a second child than the first. After all, the best name's already taken, right? At least for the girl, in our case. Bryan's got just one name in mind for a boy and appears close-minded to all of the terrific, really fabulous names I come up with. I think his choice is too common. He doesn't think so. He says I got to name the first child, so he gets to name the second. I have to remind him we're not naming our fish.

Besides, I didn't name the first. I merely came up with the name, and he liked it. Furthermore, four years earlier he got to pick out the minister for our wedding—somebody I barely knew but somebody with whom he often played tennis. On top of that, my friends and I once rolled this particular minister's house. I certainly would have exercised better discretion had I known Bryan would choose *him* to marry us.

DAY 12

Here's a good litmus test to see if you're ready to have a second child:

Have the first child (which is a prerequisite to having a second). Take said child—preferably four years and under—

with you *by yourself* on an eight-hour, nonstop drive, during which time you're experiencing a nasty bout of morning sickness and overall extreme sluggishness.

If you still have your sanity after such a trip, then you're not ready.

DAY 13

Today is Father's Day.

My father will never know of the grandchild I'm carrying in my womb. He barely knew Courtney. He passed away three months ago after a sudden heart attack.

But my children will know my father. When they're older, I will tell them all about him. All about how their grandfather was a talented painter, wood-carver and photographer. I'll show them the priceless works of art that adorn—and warm—our house. All about his keen sense of detail that was the foundation of his creativeness. All about how he had that special off-beat sense of humor evident in his fondness for *Pink Panther* cartoons and *Get Smart* reruns. All about how he, a Christian man, always tried to find the good in people, not their faults.

All about how he was a wonderful father to me.

DAY 14

I'm having a love affair with a box of saltines.

Between these delicious encounters (crackers is all I can stomach the last few days), I found time to go to the zoo with my mother and my two-year-old daughter. So the first thing that comes to mind is the old pregnant wives' tale about expecting mothers going to a zoo and viewing ugly animals. I scoff.

But I didn't scoff at my morning sickness today. I came across a sign about antelopes—which was spelled "antilopes."

I turned to my mother and said, "They misspelled antelope. I have to sit down." Typographical errors don't usually make me sick to my stomach. Actually, all I made was two totally unrelated statements back to back.

"You *smell* antelope and have to sit down?" my mother questioned.

Courtney didn't say anything. She was too busy wondering how anyone could misspell antelope.

I leave the stroller with Mom and struggle for fresh air in a section of the zoo they call "Valley of the Cats." I lean over a railing and suddenly hear the screeching of a couple of cougars nearby.

"Fight! Fight!" I excitedly tell Mom and Courtney. I temporarily forgot about my morning sickness.

We catch up to what turned out to be two amorous cougars involved in their own "encounter."

I wonder if cougars get morning sickness.

DAY 15

Special long-ago feelings rush to the present when you go home for a visit. Those feelings seem even further in the past when you take your toddler and introduce her to all the places and things you grew up with.

Memories and the present don't always match. The backyard, where I once played football with the neighborhood boys as a kid, has shrunk. Maples and other hardwoods, on the other hand, seem so much taller as their long shadows drape across our quiet dead-end street. Courtney and I walk down the street; she seems more interested in pebbles and small sticks that line the pavement.

Only a few names on the mailboxes are recognizable. Just the names of the parents of the kids I grew up with—kids who are no longer kids but who are now the parents.

DAY 16

It's amazing the things a parent will do in the name of self-preservation.

Take that eight-hour, nonstop drive I mentioned a few days ago. Surviving this trip was the number-one thing on my mind as my two-year-old and I were returning from a visit to Nashville to see my mom.

The key to this survival is knowing where all of the McDonald's Playland restaurants were along the interstate. Not just any McDonald's—the ones with the big slide, wrap-around tunnel, and trampoline full of colorful balls.

Secondly, the prepared parent has a well-stocked supply of cassette tapes to entertain the child and will not lose his/her temper when all the child wants to listen to is something called "Rock With Barney," an approximately twenty-four-minute sing-along that features a purple, environmentally correct dinosaur and a handful of talented children who sing "Yankee Doodle Dandy" and "Ain't It Great To Be Crazy?" to snappy beats. Hearing those tunes for about six hours and forty-five minutes of the trip was enough to drive me crazy. But then I discovered an unlikely alternative: disco.

Those snappy beats from the '70s (I'm thankful for K-Tel) kept Courtney entertained when I refused to play another beat of Barney tunes. She especially likes "Disco Inferno," "I'm Your Boogie Man," (is Boogie Man one word or two?), "More Than A Woman," and here's my favorite—"I Will Survive."

DAY 17

Family.

It's the backbone of America. It's the solid foundation that inspires greatness in individuals. It's the element that instills moral fibers during the precious, formulative years.

It's also the people who can drive you crazy when you have more family on the way.

Take grandmas, for example. Well, actually, they're not your grandmothers, but rather they are moms, either yours or your husband's, who go through a mysterious metamorphosis the moment you conceive. In fact, grandmas always know when you conceive. even though you do not.

As a result of this change, a grandma ceases to use the nasty ten-letter word, "discipline," in favor of a more pleasant-sounding word with only five letters, "spoil." She has totally forgotten her own child-rearing days when a day didn't pass without at least one of her children being 1) spanked, 2) sent to the corner, 3) made to have his/her mouth washed out with soap, 4) grounded (that one's my favorite), or 5) all of the above.

This is something you have to take into consideration whether this is your first or tenth child—because there is a price to be paid. That price isn't evident until that first visit by your child *alone* with grandma. The longer the visit, the higher the price. It's not that grandma charges you to keep your baby. Rather, it's the spoiling that's quite taxing on mom and dad because mom and dad have to "undo" grandma's spoiling.

I call it "debriefing the baby." Put the baby under bright lights and heavy interrogation, and in a matter of a few days to a few weeks—depending on the length of time grandma had the baby in her sole clutches—the baby becomes unspoiled and back to normal.

Has your baby been excessively spoiled by grandma? Simply note the clear-cut signs:

• Whining
• Back-talking
• Wanting to be held more than usual
• Whining and back-talking because you're not holding him/ her more than usual

The "grandma-withdrawal" symptoms are not too much different than that of a recovering addict. Remember, it's your persistence, diligence and "tough love" that'll bring your baby back to reality.

Until the next visit with grandma.

DAY 18

Went to see *Batman Returns* today.

I forgot what it's rated, PG or PG-13. However, I'd like to submit my own rating for this popular flick: WMS-68.

That is, Women with Morning Sickness before the 68th day of gestation need to cautioned as this movie contains gross scenes.

The grossest of all was where Penguin waddles down a flight of stairs gnawing on a raw fish when he's asked to run for mayor of Gotham City. Then, Penguin gets irate, and with flecks of meat clinging to his ugly chin, viciously bites a campaign worker's nose.

There are other movies that should be rated WMS-68:

• *Alien* (Remember the Alien-out-of-the-stomach incident?)

• *Nightmare on Elm Street* (Freddie without the mask makes this one gross enough to make our list.)

• *The Howling* (Recall the famous line, "I'll give you a piece of my mind!")

• *Friday the 13th, Parts I through XLVIII*

• *The Brady Bunch* reruns, especially *The Brady Bunch Variety Hour*. (Okay, I know that's not a movie, but those shows should be avoided anyway. Watching a perm-topped Greg is a definite no-no during early pregnancy!)

DAY 19

After giving it considerable thought, I've decided Eve is not my favorite Bible character.

It has to do with that stunt she pulled in the Garden of Eden that utimately resulted in my 'round-the-clock morning sickness. It was bad enough a week or so ago when it was just two main waves of sickness—mid-morning and dusk.

If Eve were here today, I'd tell her a thing or two. To begin with, I'd tell her to shelve the fig leaves for something a bit more fashionable for the '90s, like Gitanos or even something from the Jaclyn Smith line at Kmart. Then, after she was presentable, I'd let her know how much I don't appreciate the annoying inconveniences of being pregnant.

For one thing, my husband and daughter probably don't enjoy my wild mood swings. And I don't particularly enjoy those four-inch-long vitamin pills I have to take each morning to supplement the nutrients I don't get from my Doritos. (Bryan puts the pill in the straw and blows in my direction as I open my mouth, choke down the pill, and suddenly get an overwhelming urge to neigh.)

Of course, we don't know what childbirth and the preceding nine months would've been like had Eve not eaten the forbidden fruit and encouraged Adam to do the same.

However, we can speculate. First of all, there wouldn't be such a thing as "weight gain." The baby would receive all the nourishment he/she needs and grow normally, but all this activity inside the womb would not cause any external bulges. And you could forget about morning sickness, mood swings, leaky breasts, maternity clothes, bad perms, and Monistat-7 commercials. Further, you could tie your shoes and shave your legs in the shower (not necessarily at the same time) at any time during pregnancy. Then, when it was time to give birth, just wiggle your nose like Samantha, and poof, there's the baby!

Oh well, time to snap out of The Garden and take another spoonful of Emetrol.

DAY 20

I've been thinking about pregnancy myths a lot lately. Many are so silly as we approach the twenty-first century. Things like, if a pregnant woman attends a funeral she'll have a marked baby. Or, if she listens to Chopin during her pregnancy, she'll be assured of a child with exceptional musical talent. Or, if a pregnant woman steps on a crack, it'll break her mother's back.

There are other not-so-known myths that loom over pregnant women. Here's my favorite: a pregnant woman gains between twenty and twenty-five pounds during pregnancy.

Yeah, right.

When my doctor told me that one, not only did I get a good chuckle, but also I filed that bit of info with the Never-Eat-Raisin-Bran-While-Facing-East-On-The-Third-Tuesday-Of-Your-Fourth-Month-If-A-Squall-Line-Is-Approaching-From-The-Northwest myth (which, by the way, results in a baby high in fiber with a good sense of direction and a promising future as a meteorologist).

DAY 21

When I was pregnant the first time around, I couldn't get my hands on enough pregnancy books. The second time around, some women shun all the pregnancy propaganda and go on memory. Well, I think it's important to reread all the information from nutrition to fetal growth—it's vital for your own well-being and the health of your child.

One thing that's bothered me as I'm being refreshed with pregnancy propaganda: those drawings of women's tummies depicting the different stages of pregnancy. Have you noticed how *flat* the stomach is during the first and second months? My stomach under normal, non-pregnant conditions represents the convex tummy in the third-month illustration.

I guess I'm just ahead of my time.

DAY 22

I remember when I was pregnant with Courtney everybody else was pregnant, too. Yet, *I* was the first and only one going through it at the time. Once I had Courtney, everybody else stopped being pregnant, too. They all had babies the same age as my daughter—no matter how old she was…and is.

Well, everybody's pregnant again. Only this time they all have two-year-olds. Which brings up a pressing issue not prevalent during the first pregnancy.

Potty training.

Unless your husband has his own toilet problems, you probably didn't have potty concerns the first time around. Now the potty-training dilemma is all-consuming, as the thought of paying double for disposable diapers is scary.

We introduced the porta-potty to Courtney on her year-and-a-half birthday back in November with no intention of beginning this venture until she turned two.(We actually tried to get a Port-O-John, the kind construction workers use, but it wouldn't fit into the bathroom.) Anyway, we made a big deal out of the potty introduction with an authentic potty party that included hors d'oeuvres (Oreos and apple juice). We invited the governor, but he had other commitments.

She screamed and ran out of the bathroom as soon as we lifted the lid.

I think she was expecting a Port-O-John.

DAY 23

I figure I'm about six weeks along now. Thus, the countdown has started until my curves stop curving in and begin to curve out. What this means is that I'm wearing as much figure-flattering apparel as I can to reveal my concave (sorta) waist. I've been toying with the idea of a last-minute trip to Victoria's Secret.

Perhaps it's a sign of denial that I'm going to get big again, that I'll be forced to wear elastic waistbands, not to mention those stupid-looking pouch slacks and tent-size jumpers.

I stashed all of the maternity garb in a plastic trash bag that sits in the corner of my closet. I didn't bother to even fold them properly when I was finished with them the first time. So I guess I'll need an iron, which makes digging out these fashionable clothes even less appealing.

In view of this, what *does* become appealing are my sweats. In fact, I still wear the black sweat pants I was wearing when my water broke the first time around. I think I washed them.

I'm sure I didn't iron them, though.

DAY 24

The 'round-the-clock morning sickness seems to have subsided, at least a little bit. That's a relief, although the Emetrol people were beginning to see me as their ticket to a huge Christmas bonus this year.

I've also gained back the two pounds I lost since the dot appeared nearly a month ago. Maybe I'm just retaining water.

Actually, I've been retaining a strange appetite. Two nights this week I dished up hard-boiled eggs with side dishes of macaroni and cheese and grilled cheese sandwiches for supper. The pregnancy experts caution against eating raw eggs. I'd caution against it, too, pregnant or not. But here's where the raw eggs thing hits close to home.

Homemade ice cream.

That's right, pregnant women ought not eat homemade ice cream. And I suspect that rules out uncooked Tollhouse cookie dough, too.

So how am I expected to gain weight?

DAY 25

Want to know the ingredients to a bad mood?

• Morning sickness makes another appearance after you thought it was history.

• Your two-year-old throws a 10-minute tantrum in the checkout line at the grocery store when you tell her she can't have a Nilla Wafer until it's paid for. Then during said tantrum folks over sixty-five who are allergic to tantrums gather around to ask her if she's being mistreated.

• The aforementioned two-year-old then refuses to take a nap.

• The morning sickness lingers on.

• Your perm just isn't cooperating.

• A marketing representative sends you a letter denying a $1.25 refund for purchasing a particular brand of diapers.

Now if you have a toddler who has not made it to the potty, you know the importance of diaper coupons. After all, we are in the midst of the "diaper wars" as the last of the baby boomers are busting out with babies.

I usually stick with the $1 off coupons that I cash in at the register, as I'm too busy to remember to fill out a form, cut out a proof of purchase thing, find a stamp, find an envelope, address it, and head out to the mailbox.

But this time I did. And after all that trouble and expense, I was denied the whopping $1.25 because the offer had expired. They were right; it had—although only a week or so. Nevertheless, I fumed over this, in principle mainly. And principal secondly.

I also felt like sending this marketing person a curt letter. Curt wouldn't do it so I wrote it myself. In a nutshell, I told her that my opinion of her diaper company had changed totally (not that I had really given much thought to this company before). Had she refunded my money regardless of the fact that I was tardy in sending the coupon in, I would have really been impressed. Instead, I told her I was boycotting her product because of the lack of customer interest her company displayed.

These diaper companies know all about you. From the time of conception (and they know better than you when that was), they're sending you all sorts of coupons and incentives to buy their products. So this omniscient marketing rep probably thinks it's no big deal because my two-year-old will be in rubber pants any day now.

What she doesn't know is baby makes four, and future money from me to her company is none.

DAY 26

This is the first time I've been pregnant on Independence Day. There's something ironic about that statement.

One thing I'll always remember about this day is the number of times I made the declaration that I had to go to the bathroom during the night. Well, I declared it to myself three different times as I rushed from the bed to the bathroom in the nick of time. It made Bryan declare it to himself, too, and he promptly followed suit one or two of those times. He's really empathetic, as I've already noted, and not one to be upstaged.

But all this declaring has me worried. Why? Because I'm supposedly a normal, red-blooded, healthy American woman, and normal healthy American women don't typically dream about going to the bathroom. The dreams were so vivid, they came to life. The going-to-the-bathroom plots seem to have overtaken my sleep-time habits.

I realize I'm supposed to be making frantic trips to the bathroom at all hours of the day—and night—because of the baby. And I'll see more of the same as the third trimester approaches. I don't know why it's not such a nuisance during the second trimester—maybe you're just used to it by then.

DAY 27

One of my favorite pairs of pants is getting tight around the waist.

This is disturbing. I remember with Courtney it was the third month or so when things started to get a bit snug. And I know

I'm not that far along yet. Actually, I lost a pound that I earlier gained back after losing it to begin with. I guess I'm retaining water.

Nope. I'm afraid I'm going to have to face reality and accept the fact that I'll probably show earlier with this one. I'll just have to brace myself for that event even though I don't think I'm ready to trade in my Aigner belt for an elastic waistband.

DAY 28

Here's some advice on how to cut down on middle-of-the-night trips to the bathroom: Don't eat a bowl of squash for dinner and a piece of watermelon for dessert. Who would've known? That feast in itself is 153.7 percent water.

So I was busy during the night, as usual. But I've had some strange cravings lately, and believe me, nobody joined me in that meal. Bryan and Courtney ordered takeout.

On a brighter side, I'm beginning to experience those dreams that normal, red-blooded, healthy thirty-year-old American women have.

That's right. Golf dreams.

I was the envy of all other normal healthy thirty-year-old American women as I shot a forty on the front nine of a lush, well-manicured, semi-private course in the mountains of Roanoke, Virginia. It was something worth drooling over. But I never got to the back nine.

Why? For the same reason the pros don't eat squash before a tournament.

DAY 29

I got a nice compliment today. A lady I never met, never saw before, and probably will never see again said I look real good for being pregnant—even just two months pregnant. Of course, she didn't know what I looked like before.

Such a statement could've been risky on her part. But I took it as a compliment because although I'm not showing yet, I feel like I am. And I should be although I don't want to yet. It's kind of like being sick and taking your temperature only to find out you don't have one. You're still just as sick, but there's no tangible proof.

Perhaps the only tangible proof I have at the moment is my failing perm. There's a distinguishable line between the permed and unpermed, some famous person once said. And my perm has become frizzy, making it somewhat unmanageable. Can I blame unruly hormones that have taken over my body? Can I blame the unruly hairdresser who gave me the perm to begin with? Can I blame time, as it's been three months since I got the perm?

What's a pregnant woman with no scapegoat to do?

DAY 30

Strange veins have begun to protrude along my shins. I don't know if they're the varicose ones or not. I've been told to watch for those during pregnancy. Actually, I've been told not to cross my legs because that causes them, too, whether I'm pregnant or not. I've also been told to wash colors inside out so they won't fade.

But it's important to be careful when you're pregnant. Listen to the old mom's tales, but take them with a grain of salt or salt substitute. Research what people tell you, talk to your doctor, and read as much as you can, because for nine months you're solely responsible for that little one you're carrying in your womb.

That's kind of scary.

It's also one of the most rewarding things you'll ever do—whether it's your first, second, or tenth child.

So what's a little vein protrusion when it comes to giving life?

Second Month

DAY 31

Well, it's been a month since we found out we're pregnant. This "we" stuff is so popular nowadays when discussing pregnancy because it lets the husband feel like he's involved. Helps the proverbial male ego.

Anyway, a lot has happened these past thirty days. Let's review:

• I learned, to my surprise, that *any* shade of purple indicates a "Baby Will Soon Be On Board."

• Workouts continue (and I still look good in my Spandex).

• Bryan and I experienced priceless moments when Courtney told us she's going to be a big sister.

• On expert advice, I avoided kitty litter.

• With the aid of gallons of Emetrol, I survived the peak of morning sickness—in spite of that gross scene in *Batman Returns*.

• Cracker stock went up several points during aforementioned morning sickness.

• We cogitated over names that would be fitting with Nutt.

• I looked up the word "cogitated" to see what it means.

• I've faced the realization that my pants are getting somewhat snug, although it probably has less to do with being pregnant and more with retaining water. Besides, my pants always shrink in the wash.

The next month, I'm sure, is sure to build on these climactic events.

DAY 32

As a pregnant member of society, I don't really realize my limitations until I go to a fair.

First of all, the odors of steak kabobs, funnel cakes and barbecue pork sandwiches blend to create an atmosphere where it's best for a woman under the influence of morning sickness not to inhale. Secondly, just *watching* the swirling rides adds to this queasiness—riding these rides, of course, is a no-no. That includes bungee jumping, too. Third, have you ever noticed the type of people who come out of the woodwork to attend these things? I mean, besides normal people like you and me. I don't have to tell you that observing these people isn't a good idea if you wish to conquer the morning sickness.

But there are things I can do—and did, last night at the Salem Fair in Salem, Virginia. Probably the highlight was the armadillo race. All I could think about was how it probably hurts Momma armadillo when she gives birth with all that armor. Then there was the petting zoo—goats, a zebu, sheep, rabbits, chicks, and even a pot-bellied pig. And we saw a camel and an elephant. I think Courtney was disappointed, however; she was hoping to see a dog.

We had fun, and we saved money because I couldn't do much. We spent two bucks on soft drinks, and that was it. Bands and puppet shows entertained us.

And so did the weird people.

DAY 33

I feel like the clock has been turned back fifteen years.

I don't know if it was that Three Musketeers bar I ate a few days ago or if it was the small order of French fries from the Golden Arches I consumed recently.

It's probably pregnancy.

That's right. I've seemed to sink back into the days of puberty since I'm now experiencing one of those aggravating things that torments most teenagers.

A pimple.

This particular pimple is quite noticeable. It didn't emerge from behind my left earlobe or even at the beginning of my hairline where my permed bangs could subtly conceal it. Nope. It's one of those directly-under-the-right-nostril pimples. I guess that's why Bryan hasn't kissed me the last sixteen and a half hours. And I don't blame him.

I guess that's why so much of adolescent smooching is done at night, in the dark, and with both participants' eyes closed. Absolutely no smacky-mouth would be accomplished if it were left only to those who are pregnant.

DAY 34

I reckon my days of denial are numbered.

Well, not *denial* exactly. More like not-facing-up-to-the-fact-I'm-gonna-get-big-whether-I-like-it-or-not problem.

Last night as I was readying for my shower, I noticed it for the first time.

The "pooch."

No, we don't have a dog. Well, we do have seven fish—it used to be more than that, but there have been several fatalities in our tank lately. But that's another story. Rather, the pooch I'm talking about is what every mother-to-be goes through as her girth grows. It's no wonder why my pants are getting tight around the waist.

Secondly, I gained back the lone pound I had lost in the

beginning but never regained until this morning. In case you're keeping a log of my weight, I lost two pounds since finding out I'm pregnant, and about a week or so ago I gained one of those back. I'm not sure which one though. This morning the scales refused to tip in my favor, and thus, the long-lost pound resurfaced, only to push that red needle a smidgen to the right. Although it's just a smidgen to those non-pregnant types who count everything on "weight fluctuation," to the woman in early pregnancy, it signifies so much more.

There will be no fluctuation to the left for the next seven months.

DAY 35

Today I made one of the most difficult decisions I've had to make since becoming pregnant.

But I know it's the right one, Baby! Uh huh!

I decided to quit playing singles for the season and just stick with doubles. I'm talking tennis here. The temps have been soaring past the ninety-degree mark for the last week or two, and frankly, that just gets plum dangerous for a lot of people, especially pregnant women. This is regardless of how good in shape you are, too.

I must keep in mind that if my body overheats, the baby's will, too. And for a baby that's just two months old and in the crucial developmental months, it's crucial I keep myself in safe conditions.

I wouldn't take my two-year-old out in this heat and play her three sets. Not only is that motherly instinct, but it's also horse sense.

I don't think I'd play a horse three sets, either.

So this motherhood thing consumes your entire being; perhaps not at the point of conception for all women, but definitely soon after as the need to protect the unborn—in my case, from my own lifestyle of playing competitive tennis—becomes overwhelming. It would go against nature for me to continue playing in the fervent manner I typically do.

I guess that's why I don't understand pregnant women who

drink alcohol or do drugs or smoke. To continue these potentially dangerous lifestyle habits puts the baby at an unnecessary risk for a number of problems and even for death.

That's not what nature intended.

DAY 36

Pregnancy can sure make you do some strange things.

Take right now, for example. I'm eating Fig Newtons and watching *Gidget*. That's the original *Gidget* with Sally Field before she turned in her surfboard for a nun's habit. Not that later series where Gidget's all grown up married to that Moon Guy (wasn't it Moon Mullins?) and with a daughter or niece or somebody related to her. Everybody knows Gidget is an eternal teenager. Kind of like Dick Clark. No one ever came up with a series where Dick grew up, got married, had kids, made a budget, or did anything besides introducing The Rolling Stones or New Kids on the Block on his *Bandstand*. There are just some things you can't improve upon. Which, by the way, is why *The Brady Bunch Variety Hour* didn't fly.

So what does all this have to do with being pregnant?

Not much. Except that it makes me think some strange thoughts.

DAY 37

Not only have I been more keenly aware of pregnant women around me now that I'm pregnant again, but I am also paying more attention to those who are a step ahead of me setting the example: juggling a toddler and an infant.

And maintaining their sanity (or at least, what's left of it).

I've got some good friends who are in that baby boat, and I'm constantly prying for information on how they're managing. It's important to seek out answers and learn from others.

Through my preliminary investigation, I learned:

• Losing the extra weight after the second one is tons easier than after the first because you're twice as busy tending to two rather than one.

• It's more difficult to find bonded baby-sitters willing to work for a mere $13.75 an hour to watch your brood.

• Your idea of having a romantic evening alone with your husband is about as feasible as Cindy Crawford modeling bellbottom pants and clogs for the fall line.

• Having money that you haven't already spent on formula and diapers for the aforementioned romantic evening—somewhere besides McDonald's, that is—is equally ridiculous.

• You forget your husband's name and vice versa, referring to each other only as "Daddy" and "Mommy." (Hey, this happened to Ronald Reagan, and his kids are grown now.)

• You start arranging your daily schedule around *Sesame Street*.

That's about all I can handle for now. My conclusion is that I need to make the most out of these next seven months.

DAY 38

I think it's important to note that I've lost those two pounds again.

And I can still fit into my tennis skirt.

To top off all this good news, I haven't had morning sickness for more than a week now.

But it's weird. The pooch is still prominent. I've been keeping a close vigil on my bellybutton.

I should get a life.

But during my first pregnancy the bellybutton mysteriously disappeared. It's one of those oddities you read about in *Time-Life* books. So what happens to the bellybuttons? I do know there have been reported cases of bellybutton sightings in an EconoLodge in southwestern Missouri.

Or is that where folks have spotted Elvis?

Not exactly on the subject, but I've heard that Elvis lost his bellybutton in 1974.

Anyway, to get back on topic...some pregnant women experience the bellybutton metamorphosis. That is, their "innies" gradually get shallower and shallower until they ultimately disappear. Then, a week or two later they reappear in the form of "outies." Accompanying all this activity is the emergence of dark, vertical stretch marks.

So maybe I won't get any cover photo calls from *Cosmopolitan* after my seventh month.

But then again, there's always *Science Digest*.

DAY 39

The oddities continue.

First of all, did you know Fannie Flagg was in *Grease*? Here's the other oddity for the day: I actually watched that movie tonight.

Furthermore, the ending made me sad. Tears welled up in my eyes as the Rydell High School seniors bade farewell at the graduation carnival (right after Olivia Newton-John profoundly proved to the world that the only way to get a guy is to look trashy).

Grease wasn't a sad movie. *Grease 2*, on the other hand, made me cry. Some actresses-to-be in their early careers do unscrupulous things, like appearing in magazines buck-naked or just naked, but Michelle "Catwoman" Pfieffer sunk even lower: starring in that flop. You know she must be embarrassed now that has come to light.

Anyway, my point is that the weirdest things make me sad nowadays: *The Wonder Years*, Wimbledon, The Weather Channel, Monistat-7 commercials. I guess it's my hormones on the fritz again, joining the current state of my perm.

Maybe it's the food I've been eating. I've heard that pizza allegedly causes strange dreams. I've also heard it causes labor to start. Now that my morning sickness seems to be history, I'm once again enjoying hearty foods from the Four Basic Food Groups: Chicken 'n' Dumplings, Popsicles, Cheetos and Fresca. (Fresca has no caffeine, by the way.) I've recently had unexplained cravings for oatmeal, too.

It's odd; nobody will dine with me.

DAY 40

Well, Bryan and I are at a stalemate concerning this give-the-baby-a-name thing.

I have the feeling the Foremans had the same sticky dilemma; his sons are named George—one Jr. and the rest with a different roman numeral following it. It's my understanding that city founders all over the country couldn't solve this same problem when it came to naming streets—1st Street, 2nd Street, 3rd Street, etc. Not to mention Main, Elm and Maple streets.

Just plain laziness.

However, Bryan and I aren't slothful. Or even slothless. We've spent endless hours coming up with names the other one doesn't like. It's not easy being obstinate, either.

The first step is admitting we have a problem. It's simple: Bryan just can't get a grip. What I mean—and I mean it with love and stuff like that—is that he doesn't share the same fondness for certain names that I know would be perfect for our unborn child.

At this point, we feel we have tons of time to come up with a name. Baby Nutt just won't do. Especially when he/she begins to collect Social Security. But I'm beginning to think we may have to go independently on this one and have Bryan choose a boy's name and me, a girl's name. The only rule being that the name the other chooses is tolerable (i.e., Bryan can't choose "Quentin" for a boy because I once had a German shepherd by that name. That sort of thing.) I'll suggest this to Bryan.

Call it The Great Compromise.

DAY 41

The morning sickness has returned, at least for a cameo appearance.

That just goes to show that once you return the Emetrol spoon to the silverware drawer, it's just tempting fate, and the morning sickness is bound to hit the stage for an encore performance.

Kind of like *The Return to Gilligan's Island*.

Actually, all those shows where they reunite most of the original cast members decades after the show has been banished to Rerun Dungeon are really depressing. Everybody looks old. They may not be old—that's all a state of mind anyway—but you end up comparing them to what they looked like in the black-and-white days. And then you think about how you were three years old when Opie juggled taking piano lessons from Clara and playing quarterback for his football team, and then got Arnold to sub for him at the ivories when Aunt Bea wasn't noticing.

Then *you* feel old.

Old or not, this morning sickness is getting out of hand. I'm a tolerant person to a point, and I'm close to reaching that limit.

Mainly because all I feel like doing is watching reruns.

DAY 42

Today Courtney burped and immediately said, "Excuse me."

I couldn't have been more proud if she were named a Rhodes Scholar.

Two thoughts here:

1) Okay, maybe not a Rhodes Scholar. How about top two percent of her Harvard Law School graduating class?

2) The rewards a mother reaps sometimes come in strange forms, as in this case, gas.

I have worked with Courtney since she uttered her first "da-da" (they never say ma-ma first, do they?) to instill good manners and polite words into her speech patterns. She's gotten pretty good with "please" although she sometimes uses it for "thank you."

And always on command.

"What do you say, Courtney?" I ask her after she receives a piece of candy from a friend at church.

"Please," she replies.

"Well, yes, that's fine and proper, dear, but what do you say *after* he gives you the candy?" I inquire.

"Thank you," she responds, as if I pulled a string with a white plastic ring on the end of it to make her speak like something from Mattel.

The candy-giving friend smiles.

So Courtney's got a good memory and is tops on repetition. And perhaps she doesn't fully understand what she's repeating. But one day she will. After all, she excused herself after burping without me reminding her to excuse herself. That's the first step.

In the meantime, I'll just bask in my reward.

DAY 43

I gave in.

I told Bryan what I thought about a few days ago: he can choose the boy's name and I, the girl's.

I won this battle.

Perhaps it's in the guise of a compromise, but my victory stems from my gut feeling (no, not morning sickness again) that I know it's a girl.

Or rather, *she's* a girl.

At eight or nine weeks along, I certainly don't *know* whether I'm carrying a boy or a girl. And by eight or nine months, I don't expect to *know* either.

But I still know.

Just a feeling, I guess. And the fact that Bryan wants a boy—although he'd love another girl just the same, and his number one hope is that he or *she* is healthy.

Many couples opt to find out the sex of their child. I say it's none of their business, especially after the child is married, and what goes on behind closed doors is of a private nature.

I hope.

Concerning gender, however, I think it kind of spoils the climactic event of birth—that moment, which seems like an eternity, when the doctor pulls him or *her* out and announces whether it's a boy or a girl or both. Twins, that is. Before that time, it's fun to wonder what you'll have and hear more old moms' tales about if you're carrying high it's a boy and if low it's a girl, or maybe I have that one backwards.

Economically speaking, it's probably wise to find out what's in the womb. Obviously, you can start purchasing the gender-style diapers in advance (but, of course, if you use cloth that's not a problem to begin with). And if you're having what you already have, you just need to dig out the outgrown clothes you already have for what you're going to have.

However, hardly any ultrasound picture of the womb is conclusive. They can be probable, but not decisive. Which means you're possibly setting yourself up for a letdown. Or a big, pink monkey wrench could get thrown into your baby blue nursery all set up for Baby Billy's arrival.

Nah, I think it's best—for us—not to know. We do want to know when it's born, though.

Or rather, when *she's* born.

DAY 44

Matches in my tennis skirt are numbered.

Actually, my *matches* are probably numbered. This weekend I played in a doubles tournament, and we won the tournament, by the way, but that's not the point. It's an interesting side note, though.

Anyway, I told my partner I'd wear my tennis skirt if we made it to the finals. I typically wear baggy shorts and oversized T-shirts when I play, taking about twenty-three years off my age. So I donned the skirt, which has a non-elastic waistband which is—under nonpregnant circumstances—very loose around my waist. But now that my waist is becoming somewhat elastic, it's not as loose.

And inch by inch, this pregnancy thing is becoming very tangible.

DAY 45

For the first time in this pregnancy, I'm up a pound. At the previous count, I had lost those two fickle pounds again. But at last count, I gained three. You don't have to be a rocket scientist to figure out this mathematical equation.

The baby doesn't weigh a pound yet—unless my OB/GYN made a mathematical error and I'm really four months along. And I've been very active lately with tennis and various Courtney activities, which always burn the calories. Speaking of calories, I'm pretty sure I haven't been consuming my usual intake and much less the extra 300 or so they tell you to eat.

So why the extra pound?

I don't know, and despite my complaining about gaining, I don't care. Last pregnancy, I made a concerted effort not to gain and ended up gaining much more than what the docs recommend. Courtney was well-nourished in the womb and came out healthy and, thankfully, still is. They further note that underweight moms put their unborn babies at risk.

In essence, what I learned from my first pregnancy that I hope to implement this time is not to worry so much about my weight. I'll worry about losing it after the baby's born. It'll probably take time like it did the first time, but the end product of a healthy baby will be worth the temporary inconvenience.

When you weigh the evidence, it's best to do what's best for your baby.

DAY 46

Why is it that doctors' scales always weigh you more than what you *really* weigh?

That's the question for today, although I mentioned in passing earlier that I'd stop worrying about my weight while I'm pregnant. I'm not worrying, just curious why I weigh four pounds more on those high-tech digital scales that measure down to the one thousandth of a pound than on my $9.95 pink bathroom scale I bought at a popular discount store. (It's popular because it carries bathroom scales that weigh you four pounds less than at the doctor's.)

I've come up with several possible explanations. None of which are too scientific. First of all, at home I weigh early in the morning, before breakfast, without my shoes on, with only my nightshirt on, after I've clipped my fingernails, after I've combed my hair, and after I've blown my nose.

I believe in achieving an accurate reading.

But at the doctor's, I've usually already eaten, the nurses won't let me take off my shoes and street clothes, my nails have grown back, new hair has grown back in, and I get all stuffed up by the time I get to the clinic. To top it off, today when I got weighed at the doctor's I was carrying a receipt in my pocket for groceries I bought earlier—a week's worth, so it was a long piece of paper. Oh yeah, I was chewing a stick of gum, too.

Doctors just don't figure in these crucial factors.

DAY 47

Got a new due date today.

After a careful study of my sonagram, my OB/GYN determined I'm not as far along as he initially thought. When he couldn't detect a heartbeat through the er, sthesoscope...stesthosope...stethoscope (I always have trouble pronouncing and spelling that hearing instrument used in auscultation), he went for the sonagram to measure the baby and "see" the heartbeat.

If weight gain doesn't make pregnancy seem tangible, watching your own child on a screen while he or she is inside you certainly will.

Although we had sonagrams done on Courtney, it's not something that's "old hat" the second time around. It's just as special when a new life begins to take form. And that form—at ten weeks (not the twelve the doc thought)—is mainly head. Then there's a short stubby torso and legs that are beginning to take shape. A crown view revealed the emergence of ears.

Bryan and I explained to our two-year-old what was on the "TV"—her tiny brother or sister. She seemed disappointed. I think she was expecting Big Bird.

The doctor then gave us a copy of what we saw on the screen, and Bryan couldn't wait to take it back to the office to show his colleagues. He did the same thing after we got a picture of Courtney at eight months in the womb—the difference being that at eight months along, she resembled a Rorschach test more than a baby. At ten weeks, the baby looks more like a baby than a blob. Still, with Courtney's sonagram picture we pointed out various parts as best as we remembered the doc telling us and as best as we could figure out.

Blob or baby, we're just as proud as parents can be.

DAY 48

Going on the monthly doctor visits is a lot more adventurous than the first time around.

The main thing is that Courtney was a lot easier to handle as a fetus than as an obstinate two-year-old.

But here are some helpful hints a mother can heed to make these trips to the OB/GYN less stressful and more enjoyable:

1) Bring the father along.

2) Bring a diaper bag jam-packed with goodies along. (Courtney particularly likes Diet Cherry 7-Up and Ritz crackers, but your child may be different.)

3) Bring your child's favorite snuggle thing. (Courtney has this little white (well, it *was* white, now it's gray) stuffed lamb that looks like it has the mange due to the wear and tear. We try to keep it out of public view as much as possible for fear the Health Department will see this thing.

4) Bring books. Actually, Courtney doesn't read the books we bring for her, but it makes us feel better if we bring them anyway.

5) Make sure your child has been adequately fed, bathed, clothed, and freshly diapered (if applicable) before arriving at the doctor's.

6) And finally, do not schedule an appointment during naptime—yours or your child's.

DAY 49

A word about naps.

Well, maybe more than one. Naps are those times you despise as a playful, fun-loving child but cherish as a hard-working, stress-ridden adult.

And simply, they are those times you *gotta* have when you're pregnant.

Sometimes I feel guilty when I take a nap, especially when I'm not pregnant. Since I've been pregnant, I haven't felt guilty. I realize the thirty-minute to one-hour snooze I take during Courtney's two- to three-hour snooze is a must in order for me to have a healthy baby. And for that baby—and Courtney—to have a well-rested mommy.

After all, naps are going to be on the endangered activities list—if not on the extinct list—once Number Two is born.

So I gotta catch them while I still can.

DAY 50

Just got through with another guiltless nap. Well, actually, I didn't sleep, but I did get some well-deserved rest.

So now I'm fresh to ponder a few things. For example, who was that girl who played the back of Patty Duke's head when she talked to her identical cousin on *The Patty Duke Show*? Or why does grass grow so much better in my mulch than in a patch beside my driveway where it hasn't grown in three years? Or why do husbands get so grossed out over things that don't seem to faze their wives?

I was thinking about that earlier today as I was changing Courtney's 807th dirty diaper. Not that I've kept records, but I bet I've changed ninety percent of the dirty diapers that occur in this household. Bryan tackled about seven percent when:

1) I was out of town.

2) I was sick in bed with a skyrocketing temperature, sore throat, stomach ailment, excruciating headache, flu, all of the above, or any combination of the above.

The remaining three percent were taken care of by grandma, who enjoys those types of things.

Someone once said that if it were left up to men to have babies, we'd become extinct. I think the reference here is to the fact that many men have a low threshold for pain. Wives hear about that threshold nearly every day they're with their men.

Frankly, I don't think men even have the *stomach* for childbirth. I hear about Bryan's low threshold for gross stuff when he gets a quick whiff of Courtney's latest uh, er, bowel movement. Might as well be biologically correct here. Forget about how the men-who-don't-eat-quiche can hunt wild game, kill it, skin it, gut it, and whatever else you do to it. But put a dirty diaper in their path and they'll flee. And that's nothing compared to all the gross stuff that occurs in women—from periods to the placenta's grand exit after the baby's born.

All this talk of gross bodily functions calls for another spoonful of Emetrol.

DAY 51

Bryan is taking me out for a romantic dinner tonight. I don't know if he knows it's romantic. All he knows is that we have a $5 off coupon for two dinner entrees at Red Lobster and that it expires next Monday.

Maybe to him that *is* romantic.

It doesn't matter. It gives us a few hours out of the house while Courtney enjoys the company of a well-trusted baby-sitter. They usually have a good time. Amy, a high school senior, teaches Courtney all sorts of things that I, now in my thirties (ooh, that hurts!), don't know to teach her.

For example, she taught her to flap her arms and sing, "I feel like chicken tonight...chicken tonight."

So the few times a year that Bryan and I take time for a little R&R (Romance and Reduced-Price Meal), I take comfort knowing Courtney is benefiting from the experience, too.

DAY 52

It's amazing some of the things you discover just because you're a parent.

Take Mr. Rogers for instance. While the rest of the English-speaking world is watching C-SPAN or syndicated reruns of *Charles in Charge*, I'm close to my two-year-old's side glued to *Mr. Rogers' Neighborhood*.

One reason why I like *Mr. Rogers' Neighborhood* is that they put the apostrophe showing possession where it belongs. Kids notice things like that—and so do moms who were journalism majors in college. Not to get too off the subject here, but have you paid attention to how people inappropriately use the apostrophe? Like a sign that reads, "We Sell Lawn Mower's." The Lawn Mower's *what*? Or forget the whole thing totally, like "Mens" bathroom. It's refreshing to know Mr. Rogers is grammatically correct.

Lately, our PBS station has been rerunning episodes of Mr. Rogers back from 1975. The copyright date at the end of the credits really isn't necessary because Mr. Rogers' cool flared sideburns, five-inch-wide tie, and lime-green zipper sweater kind of give it away. That alone dates it before the bicentennial.

I'm trying to get to my point here, and I got sidetracked by making a fashion statement. Anyway, what I found out today that I bet everybody else doesn't know is that Mr. Rogers is married. And guess what her name is.

Mrs. Rogers. (Again, this pre-dates the women's movement that would otherwise replace the Mrs. with Ms.)

I'm just guessing, but they've probably been married for quite some time because they look alike. Only difference I could tell is that she wore these black, horn-rimmed glasses and a dress. (Her fashion statement obviously omits the wearing of zipper sweaters and Keds.)

But what struck me is the couple appears so well-rested. I mean, *too* well-rested and relaxed. Always smiling, saying cheerful things, keeping up a sweet disposition. That just leads me to one conclusion.

There aren't any Baby Rogerses.

DAY 53

I remember looking at black-and-white photographs of my mother before and after she had my older brother. She looked so much thinner. Unhealthfully so. (Is unhealthfully a word?)

She didn't have to worry about the excess weight after childbirth and she didn't have to go join a health club to work it off. The baby worked it off for her. I don't think she ever walked twelve miles to school barefooted in the snow when she was a child. But I do know she hand-cleaned cloth diapers using a bona fide washboard. (She was the talk of the neighborhood because of that one.)

There were other aspects to caring for a baby that weren't as easy then as they are now. For one thing, there are disposable diapers, costly but convenient, and from what I hear the diaper service is making a comeback because of environmental issues surrounding overcrowded dumps.

Think about baby monitors. Why, a mother back in the '50s and '60s couldn't get a decent tan for running in and out of the house constantly checking on the baby. Of course, health issues surrounding the dangers of too much sun exposure put a damper on getting a tan nowadays.

Then there's the latest advances in formula. Well, it's kind of expensive, and certainly more so than breast milk, which by the way is what's recommended anyhow.

And what about all the electronic stuff that's come out for kids that wasn't around three decades ago. Then, they had *Howdy Doody*, *Romper Room*, *The Bozo Show*. I do know Bozo's still on, but there are tons of children's programs with the advent of Cable TV and especially VCRs, so you can tape what you miss because you're busy watching something else. I don't know, it doesn't leave much time for young imaginations.

Maybe we're not really any better off now than thirty years ago—just into spending more for less.

DAY 54

It happened at our friends' house last night: I used the I'm-eating-for-two-now excuse while at an ice cream social for the first time during this pregnancy.

I think I'm a little ahead of schedule.

I had no idea it was going to happen. It was all of a sudden. My first helping of vanilla ice cream had a mere dab of caramel sauce with two, maybe three, strawberries on the side—fruit is a healthy thing. To drink: I had ice water.

Oh, I was doing so well.

Then, a friend went back for seconds. That opened the door for others who down deep desired to do the same, but secretly wanted someone else to make the initial step back toward the ice cream table.

I was a bit shy about going back and decided to wait a few extra minutes.

During that few extra minutes, the hostess obviously figured everybody was finished and put the ice cream in the freezer. Or she figured that the ice cream would melt. Or both.

As I eagerly, but unassumingly, approached the ice cream table—where the ice cream once sat—I was informed that the ice cream was indeed in the freezer.

Under nonpregnant circumstances, I wouldn't dream of bursting into my hostess's freezer and helping myself to ice cream—fish sticks, maybe, but not ice cream. But I am pregnant, and that's exactly what I did.

The morning after, I feel so ashamed. But not regretful, as I am eating for two now.

DAY 55

In just two hours, my perm will get a new look.

If that's not something to look forward to, I don't know what is. Okay, maybe I need to get out more, but my perm has gone to pot, and a fresh hairstyle should do the trick.

However, there will be no fresh perm accompanying this new hairstyle, as I heard getting perms during pregnancy—especially in the early months—is a risky investment. It could harm the baby, and it could mean big bucks down the drain if it doesn't hold what with the hormone thing and all.

After I had Courtney, as soon as I was able to drive, the first place I drove to was the salon for a perm. My hormones were getting back to normal (I'm not sure if that's good or not), and the perm looked great. But during the last trimester with Courtney, my hair looked like something from a fright movie. I couldn't wait to get a perm.

I'm sure only I thought my hair was a fright sight. Perms really aren't necessary during pregnancy, as the "glow" out-shines the rest of your features.

DAY 56

So what do you do with a two-year-old who burps during church?

For one thing, you make sure she says, "Excuse me."

(Courtney's version of "Excuse me" comes out more like "Sue me.") She did, but I don't know if she was truly penitent.

Burping during worship is something that really bothers Bryan, which is why I stopped doing it a few months after we started dating. So now he tells Courtney not to burp in church.

Like she really understands.

What Bryan seemed to overlook was the nine-year-old seated down the pew who was making lots of racket with an Incredible Hulk doll or a Ninja Turtle—I couldn't tell which, both are green with similar facial structures. He'd pull a string, and a strange buzz would infiltrate the back half of the auditorium, easily drowning out Courtney's polite burp.

But if burping's the worst thing Courtney does during that hour, I'm thankful. At her age, an hour equals two days, four hours, and thirty-seven minutes. At my age, trying to keep a two-year-old quiet and entertained during that same hour, it equals six days, fifteen hours, and four minutes.

When baby makes four, just double all of the above.

DAY 57

Nowadays thirty is not too old to have a baby, the second or the first. Careers, economics, and other factors play definite roles in this delay compared to the prior generation. June Cleaver's career was Wally and The Beaver, and Ward made a substantial income that kept the family well-fed, well-clothed, well-sheltered and, well, Ward even had extra money for a round of golf each week at the club with Lumpy's dad.

Golf costs more now, so oftentimes mom—whether she really wants to or not—must work outside the home. Some moms don't mind being away from their children during the workday as their careers motivate them to reach bigger and better goals (for them).

Many do.

In this day and time when the economy is not going to give in to the traditional family values of the '50s, it's good to see there are some families willing to sacrifice the bigger house, the fancier car, the longer vacation, and the round of golf in favor of quality time with each other.

It's been fourteen months since I quit my full-time job as a magazine editor. For a year, Courtney stayed with a member of our church during the day while Bryan and I worked to meet bills and, honestly, to get "ahead." Although we knew Courtney was in the best possible care outside of ours, it just wasn't good enough for us. We decided I should stay home with her.

It wasn't an easy decision. I don't think it's an easy decision for any woman who aspired to success in her chosen field because this decision puts her success on hold while she puts her children first.

It's a decision her children will never forget.

DAY 58

My thighs are beginning to show.

Not necessarily a pretty sight as my workouts have waned, causing my thighs to grow closer together. So I went to the "Y" for the first time in a long time this morning in an attempt to break up this "closeness."

I could tell after a few minutes on the electronic stairs contraption that a month away from all this sweat and exhaustion resulted in me sweating (pregnant women don't perspire; they sweat) and getting exhausted so much faster.

I'm not one to make excuses—usually they're already made for me; I just have to bring them up so others will know, too— but that irritating morning sickness kept me away from the gym for a long time. I did well just to play tennis once or twice a week then. Hopefully, the worst is over, and I can get on with a good exercise regimen now. For the past two days, I've managed to get in a two-mile walk.

Here's my first goal: to firm the thighs and other extremities so in a month or so, when I'm supposed to, I'll look like I'm pregnant—not fat.

DAY 59

I don't think I've recorded on paper my new due date. February 13.

Not much happened on this date, according to historians. It is Valentine's Eve. I don't know what's supposed to happen on Valentine's Eve. Love song caroling? Setting out milk and cookies for Cupid? Rushing to the card and candy shop is more like it.

On February 13, 1741, the first magazine in this country, *American Magazine, a Monthly View of the Political State of the British Colonies* (I think it was the predecessor to *Good Housekeeping*) was published in Philadelphia. It's of interest to know that this magazine, despite its "Short Story of the Month," tips on gardening, and fantastic strudel recipes, lasted only three months.

The ten-day Anchorage Fur Rendezvous, which features sled-dog races, judo, a cross-country snowmobile race, and a table tennis championship, sometimes begins on February 13. Check your Alaska paper for exact dates.

Okay, maybe February 13 is not as exciting a due date as my former one, February 2. And maybe this baby won't come out to tell us if we'll have six more weeks of winter.

But if my baby's born on February 13, it *will* be an exciting due date.

DAY 60

I must correct myself.

During a conversation with the lady who cut my hair a few days ago, I learned it may be okay to get a perm when you're pregnant after all.

But it's still a risk.

Not necessarily a risk to you or your unborn baby, but a risk to your pocketbook. Shelling out $60 for a cut, style, and perm may not be a wise investment if your hormones interfere, causing your perm to go limp before the check clears. The worst time for a perm is during the first trimester, I'm told. The best time is during the second trimester, when your body's more acclimated to being pregnant. By the time you reach the third, you're typically not feeling your best again, so it's best to wait for the bottled curls until after you give birth.

Of course, I don't know how correct all this is. My source is someone who probably wants my $60 for a "risk-free" perm.

Third Month

DAY 61

For the first time, I'm told I look pregnant by someone other than my husband.

(Actually, a male friend told me he thought I looked pregnant when I was, in reality, only three or four days pregnant—if that far along—but he says I had a "glow" about me. Of course, he tells me this *after* I tell him I am pregnant.)

Anyway, this someone other than my husband bluntly put it this way, "My, you *do* look pregnant!" This someone knows I'm not eager to look pregnant although I don't mind being pregnant (except during morning sickness). She's also someone who never did look real pregnant even in her eighth month and never looked like she just had a baby after she just had a baby.

But she's a swell friend nevertheless.

To continue, she quickly retracted her observations once she saw the look of horror on my face. (I told you she was swell.) She added, "I guess it's just because you're wearing baggy clothes." I like baggy clothes, but not baggy clothes because I *have* to wear baggy clothes.

Because then they're called maternity clothes.

DAY 62

Right now, I'm lounging by the pool, relaxing, and soaking up the mid-summer sun as Courtney takes a dip.

A dip is about all she can take in the four inches of water in her above-ground, plastic, Kmart pool that's decorated with orange-and-red bunnies. I have heard, by the way, that babies and toddlers learn to swim easier and faster than adults. Makes sense. They probably remember all that swimming they did in the womb for nine months, totaling about 9,458 miles. Of course, there's not much else to do there—except sleep, eat, and grow.

According to my sonagram, my baby is busy growing legs right now. Certainly, that will keep him/her busy for a while. Then there are the more delicate features: feet, toes, toenails. And that's just the beginning. There is so much growing to do between now and the next twenty-seven weeks that he/she won't have much time to swim.

DAY 63

I'm afraid I'm going to have to take Demi Moore off my "Moms I Look Up To The Most" list.

This month, she's appearing on the cover of *Vanity Fair* magazine in body paint.

What a tacky thing for a mom to do.

This mother-of-two is obviously afraid to show up on the cover wearing a bikini or halter top or some other tummy-revealing garment. Unlike her pregnancy cover shot. I'd have more respect for her if she did reveal her tummy than for covering it up with Temperas.

Consider: perhaps the body paint outlines the fact that she's regained her figure after two childbirths. I'm happy for her, and my congratulations card is in the mail. But the paint conceals the battle scars pregnancy creates, and these scars must be worn with pride.

That is, stretch marks.

DAY 64

When you're pregnant, you have to be careful what you do during those nine months.

At twelve weeks along, I confess I've slipped up a little.

Actually, I've done two things that I may pay for later: mow the grass and scrub the bathtub. I don't know what got into me, probably all those strange early pregnancy cravings. I don't normally mow the grass and I don't normally scrub the tub. And it's certainly too early to be "nesting," that out-of-control urge to clean the house just before the baby arrives.

What it all means is that I'm killing my excuse to do certain household tasks I could otherwise get out of. I'm cutting off my nose to spite my face.

This could be serious.

But I'm determined now not to let it get out of hand. I'll mow. I'll scrub. I'll even mop (on every other Friday that falls on the 16th of the month). However, I refuse to iron; it's too exhausting.

DAY 65

I've been holding my breath, but I think this time it's for real. The morning sickness is over.

My family is relieved, probably more than I am. Emetrol's stock dipped a few points after that shattering news.

However, it's been about two weeks since regular bouts of morning sickness, and I can still remember what it feels like. And I don't want to feel it again.

It's difficult sometimes to experience the joy of pregnancy when it's the pregnancy that makes you feel anything but joy. Now I think for the next three months or so—let's call it the second trimester—I'm going to feel pretty good, and I'm looking forward to that.

The main adjustment now is coping with the growing girth. By the way, I looked up "girth" in the dictionary. Here's what Webster's says: "2) the circumference, as of a tree trunk or person's waist."

From that, I guess you can tell how far along I am by counting the rings around my tummy.

DAY 66

Today was one of those days when I realized my own mortality.

Of course, raising a Terrible Two and being pregnant with another one who, Lord willing, will also become a Terrible Two can make you realize your own mortality.

But today, this realization did not hit me so much because of the above, but because I actually listened to "Rubberband Man" on the radio while out for my near-daily walk.

It gets worse. I cranked up the volume on my headset and briskly walked to the beat of this late '70s hit.

I guess it was a hit. I really don't remember. I think it's one of those songs on those tapes from K-Tel.

I'd like to think that my recent appetite for strange foods is to blame for this. Otherwise, I really have no excuse. Except I'm getting older. I mean, the way I see Frankie Avalon and Elvis of my parents' generation can be equated with how Courtney and her unborn sibling will view the Bee Gees and Elton John. (That's *classic* Elton—"Philadelphia Freedom," "Bennie and the Jets," etc.)

And you can tell you're getting older when you stop listening to the Top 40 stations in favor of the Lite and Easy stations. That's scary. In fact, a lot of today's new music disgusts me. For example, I really don't understand a guy who raps rebellious and seductive lyrics, pulls down his jeans, and marches around the audience in his undies. Or a woman—who's older than me, by the way—who's never satisfied with the color of her hair, does obscene things on and off stage, and hasn't learned that a bra goes *underneath* her blouse.

But what's really scary is that all this means I'm turning into my parents.

DAY 67

Today is one of those days I really don't feel like I'm pregnant.

Naturally, after two months the novelty has worn off. Everyone who is anyone knows I'm pregnant and has offered his or her own congratulatory remarks. To the naked eye, I don't look pregnant, although from my own naked body, I certainly do. Knock on wood, but I think the morning sickness is history—something only recorded in my diary and hopefully never to be experienced during this pregnancy again.

In fact, I'm feeling pretty good, which is usually a sign that the second trimester is around the corner. I must admit I've been wearing some shorts equipped with an elastic waistband. They're not maternity shorts, just a go-between to wear as my figure-flattering apparel tightens up around my slowly expanding girth—yet before I take the plunge and wear *real* maternity clothes.

DAY 68

I was able to work out today and have been regularly for the past week or so. I'm learning that it's so important to do things like that for yourself when you're pregnant. My workout doesn't take very long: twelve minutes on the step machine, twelve on the bike, and then a thirty-minute walk around the gym. If I can't make it to the "Y" to work out, then I try to take at least a two-mile walk around the neighborhood after Bryan gets home from work. (I've tried doing that taking Courtney along in her stroller—like a two-year-old really wants to stay put in a stroller!)

And exercise isn't the only thing. Without sacrificing quality time away from Courtney or from Bryan, I try to do things for myself, such as read. Right now, I'm reading five different books—from Erma Bombeck's latest title to one about the psyche of a two-year-old. Obviously, the first one is for enjoyment (Erma's my hero), and the other is for self-survival as I learn the strategy in coping with Courtney's often obstinate self.

To be a mom and do it right, you have to be selfless, but not necessarily to the point where you suffer in the process. Take care of the kids and your husband—but if you don't take care of yourself, too, then you're not worth squat to them.

DAY 69

Okay, so maybe I had seven pancakes for breakfast this morning.

That doesn't make me a pig, does it? It makes me pregnant. Well, to be biologically correct, pancakes—or any other breakfast menu item—has nothing to do with conception. However, pancakes—a whole big stack of 'em—have plenty to do with what's appetizing to me now that I am pregnant.

I must be careful, though, and not fall into the food trap I did when I was pregnant with Courtney. One of the perks of being pregnant in the first place is that you get to eat more. Three hundred calories more, to be exact. I figure that's what seven pancakes add up to—more or less.

DAY 70

I just might have to vacuum after all.

Of course, vacuuming isn't as bad as ironing, but this may become a household task I'm going to have to keep up with *daily*. That's scary.

I guess that's why folks say it's scary to sell your house and buy another—because you have to keep the carpets clean for when prospective buyers come to inspect your home. And it's not just the carpet you have to worry about. There are the windows, walls (especially if you have a two-year-old armed with a box of Crayolas), floors, and in general, keeping the house in immaculate condition.

I'm not sure I'm ready for this.

I am ready to move out of our bi-level. (Some areas of the country call it a split-level. Kind of like, here in Virginia, people say "ont" instead of "ant" for the lady who's your mom's or dad's sister. You know, aunt.) Back to what I was saying before I got sidetracked on a lesson on acceptable pronunciation, a bi-level just isn't acceptable, at least as far as having a two-year-old and another on the way is concerned. Up and down the stairs 146 times a day, more on weekends.

Maybe that's why I haven't gained weight yet.

DAY 71

So right when I gloat how I haven't gained weight (that is, going above my pre-pregnancy starting weight), I gain a pound—all just to remind me that I'm not in control of *all* the weight I have and will gain while I'm pregnant.

But there is weight I *can* and better control. A few days ago, if you'll recall, I wolfed down seven pancakes. (What I didn't mention earlier when I first told that story is that I actually put eight pancakes on my plate.) Well, exercise during pregnancy, of course, is important. So I exercised a little better self-control this morning and ate only five pancakes. These weren't very big pancakes, either.

Ideally, I should shun pancakes. It's difficult for me to curb my appetite when I put eight of them on my plate. There are other things, too, I have to stay away from:

1) Danish wedding cookies
2) Marshmallow cream-filled cookies
3) Nutter Butter cookies
4) Cookies, in general
5) Monistat-7 commercials

Staying away from the above certainly would be a good idea, but I'm not likely to take any drastic action (except maybe staying away from the Monistat-7 commercials) until after my pregnancy and the 300-extra-calorie-a-day privileges are taken away from me.

DAY 72

I received my "Fourth Month" newsletter today.

The hospital where we hope to have this baby (I say "hope"

because birthing a baby could occur anywhere…on a plane, on a train, in a box, with a fox, Sam-I-Am) sends us informative monthly newsletters on pregnancy and what to expect during the current month I'm in. Pretty neat.

This month's newsletter focuses on how it's a great month to be pregnant. (I always thought that was April.) For example, you're not quite ready for maternity clothes but your regular clothes are too tight. What's great about that? I wonder. I have to try on several outfits a day until I fit into something that doesn't make me look obscene.

But there are some great things I'll agree with: morning sickness is supposed to be over, and the urge to visit every bathroom you come within three quarters of a mile of subsides.

However, it says you're not supposed to be fatigued anymore. I've been tired since 1988, so being in the fourth month of pregnancy hasn't changed that.

DAY 73

I've made a big decision.

I'm not playing co-ed softball this fall. This decision, by the way, ranks up there with our decision to sell our house. Now I might have gone the other way had it been regular softball with just women. But when you toss men into the picture, and you have a woman—regardless of how athletic and fleet-footed she may be—who's four months pregnant playing first base, you set the stage for a possible disaster.

For one thing, I don't look real pregnant yet. I'd have to wear a sign around my neck that reads, "Don't run into me; I'm pregnant," to inform massively built men who take the game far too seriously not to flatten me as they round first base en route to second base.

So I decided to bench myself for the season.

DAY 74

Okay, it's a pregnant woman's prerogative to change her mind.

After making one of the most important decisions of my life—at least of the last two days of my life—I make a 180 and go against everything I've decided.

I've taken myself off the bench.

However, there are several stipulations. One, Bryan and I cannot play at the same time if there's no one there at the game to watch Courtney. So that should shorten my playing time a little bit. Secondly, I will take myself out if I feel threatened by massively built men rounding first or if I feel ill for whatever reason, especially for pregnancy-related reasons.

DAY 75

There's a commercial on TV where a new mom stares at her infant son and wonders aloud what the world will be like when he's her age. And then, somehow, the subject turns to disposable diapers and how this particular brand won't be a major threat to our nation's dumps and wastelands.

I'll be honest. I haven't thought as much as I should about dumps, but I have given much thought as to what things will be like when Courtney and my unborn child grow up.

And it's a scary thought, especially when you think how the world has changed over the last few decades. For example, imagine what Lucy thought the world would be like when Little Ricky grew up. Little Ricky was a product of the '60s, a decade marked by widespread drug use, newfound sexual freedom, and overall disrespect for authority.

Flip ahead a few pages to the '90s, and the picture looks bleaker. Compare the revolution of The Beatles to groups like Guns 'n Roses, or Carly Simon to Madonna. (Well, that last comparison certainly *is* weird, isn't it?)

Anyway, standards have loosened up so much that they seem to be out of control, and our children will be exposed to so much immorality—in spite of our efforts otherwise. It's scary, but it should scare us into doing our best to raise our kids in the best moral fashion possible.

DAY 76

Peace, at last—at least for a couple of days.

No offense to my two-year-old daughter and twenty-nine-year-old husband, but I needed to get away by myself for some quiet, "me" time. Courtney's staying with Grandma in Spartanburg about two and a half hours away, and Bryan's staying in Roanoke—after all, somebody has to work.

Me? I'm at a bed and breakfast inn in Dahlonega, Georgia, in the North Georgia mountains about an hour away from Atlanta. A brief history lesson here: Dahlonega was the site of our nation's *first* gold rush, which occurred in 1828—don't let those Californian forty-niners tell you otherwise.

Back to today's thought. After breakfast, I went upstairs to my room to catch up on my reading: a how-to book on selling your own home. What naturally followed was my catching up on my writing: advertisements to sell our home.

As I catch up on all this work, I'm amazed by the solitude that encompasses me. All I hear is the rhythmic pattering of the steady late summer rain on the rooftop. No *Sesame Street*. No ESPN. No whiny demands for more juice. No rattling of clothes in the dryer. No rumbling from the vacuum cleaner. (That's seldom heard in my house anyway.) No discussions between Bryan and me about who'll change Courtney's dirty diaper.

Actually, it's almost *too* quiet here.

DAY 77

One of the perks of being by yourself secluded in a bed and breakfast inn tucked away in the mountains is that you get to watch what you want on TV.

I chose one of those old movies produced in the 1700s. You know, one of those movies where bad writers come up with lines like, "You flatter me terribly." I guess that means someone did a rotten job of flattering someone to begin with. Thing is, I jumped in half-way through this movie. So I spent an hour of my precious time away from it all trying to figure out the plot. Here are some of the movie's high points:

• A father offered a glass of champagne to his daughter to

cure her headache. (Just Say No!)

• This same father discussed having an extramarital affair with a woman who strongly resembled Katherine Hepburn. (She Just Said No!)

• They end up having the affair anyway. (Nobody Said No!) I never found out if the daughter got rid of her headache, though.

DAY 78

Just got back from a walk around the "square" here in Dahlonega, buying gifts such as a T-shirt that reads, "My Mom/Wife Went To Dahlonega And All I Got Was This Lousy T-Shirt." Nah.

The walk tired me out, though, and for an athletic sort like myself, that disturbs me. Actually, I am sore from our first softball game a few days ago. That disturbs me, too. I'm disturbed easily.

So far, I'm not paranoid about being pregnant and playing first base. I did have sort of a close call, though, involving a massively built woman charging at me after hitting an infield grounder to third base. The third baseman, by the way, was my husband—very athletic but sometimes produces a wild throw to first base. On this occasion, I had to reach for this wild throw smack dab in this woman's path. This woman, I might add, was bigger than I anticipate being on the day I go to deliver. I don't think she was pregnant, however.

Motherly instinct—combined with not being the greatest first baseman ever—took over, and I got out of her way in the nick of time, allowing the wild throw to crash into the fence behind me.

It's not important that she was safe on an error, but it is important that my unborn child is safe on purpose.

DAY 79

When I was pregnant the first time, I read a lot about what it's like to be pregnant. When Courtney was born, I stopped reading.

But when Courtney evolved into a Terrible Two, a friend

whose daughter is nine months older than my daughter gave me some books that focus on this traumatic time (in the two-year-old's parents' lives, that is).

The books worked wonders, if for nothing else than to remind me there are other parents out there struggling with their offspring just like Bryan and me.

I'd even considered starting a support group, tentatively called POTT (Parents of Terrible Twos). We could develop our own 12-step program to rid ourselves of our co-dependent nature of living with a two-year-old. I had dreams of appearing on *Donahue* to spread the word of our success—assuming we were successful, of course.

But, by the time I did all that, Courtney would be at least three or maybe entering the seventh grade. So I abandoned my plans and went back to reading.

DAY 80

My brief vacation away from the rituals of everyday life has come to an end. That's what happens to all good things.

I recommend that pregnant women—especially those already with kids—take time off and away from the family. I also recommend doing all this at the bed and breakfast inn of your choice.

Where else can you sit down to breakfast with folks from across the land and discuss the hazards of being bitten by a jellyfish? (I also learned the difference between a jellyfish and a man-o'-war, in between helpings of scrambled eggs and cinnamon biscuits.)

I recommend that the bed and breakfast of your choice be in a small town, where you can while away your time swinging on the front porch and totally losing yourself in the ecstasy.

Now it's time to go back and find my family.

DAY 81

Now I'm back.

I'm spending the day reintroducing myself to my home environment—from piled-up dishes to dirty clothes. I really don't want to meet the vacuum cleaner again, though.

Actually, Bryan had the house clean when I came home. In fact, much cleaner than I left it. I don't know about you, but coming home to a clean house is a real turn-on. Based on what I've seen on TV, men often miss the boat when it comes to romance. Just stop by the store and pick up a greeting card because you care enough the send the very best and poof, the wife is putty in your hands, right?

Nope.

For one thing, you also better have a box of chocolates in *your* hands if you want in the front door, Bucko. It's not that wives are demanding or picky. It's that a visit to the store is too easy for you. True romance must be backed up with *action*. And that action should be in the form of something that makes her life a bit easier. Here are some suggestions.

- Cook breakfast.
- Cook lunch.
- Cook dinner.
- Clean up dishes after one or all of the above.
- Scrub floors.
- Iron clothes.
- Diaper the baby.
- Feed the baby.
- Do *anything* for the baby.
- And my favorite, VACUUM.

Here's what should make all this really appealing to the men: all of the above together cost less than the $7.95 box of chocolates and $1.09 card. Now that should be a real turn-on for them.

DAY 82

I've been busy getting ready to go on vacation.

I've never been pregnant on vacation before. Well, actually I have; I just didn't know I was pregnant. This time, I'm on the edge between stuffing myself in my regular clothes, including some with elastic waistbands, and opting for perhaps the more comfortable, yet not so stylish, maternity attire.

I can squeeze my growing girth into one pair of jeans and two pairs of dress pants—all three of which used to be quite loose around my former skinnier waist. My shorts are okay, especially the ones with the elastic. My tennis skirt has been retired until at least eight weeks after I give birth. My non-maternity undies are on their last legs, so to speak, as there are only a few I can wear comfortably.

This will probably be my and Bryan's last big fling before Number Two arrives, so it's important to be comfortable as I take advantage of all this relaxation that awaits us.

DAY 83

I cut Courtney's bangs for the first time.

So far, it's been a three-day process.

I probably shouldn't have started this process the very same day I trimmed the bushes in the front yard—I completed that project in an hour and a half. The difference is, however, that bushes sit still. Two-year-olds don't.

The other problem—and I'm not sure how major a problem it is—is that I'm not a professional hairstylist. I first cut her hair in the back months ago. I didn't do anything fancy, like layer it or anything. I just made the ends even.

Bangs are a different story. For one thing, Courtney loves to look at herself in the bathroom mirror as I snip, causing a lot of unexpected twisting and turning. So the bangs kept getting shorter and shorter. Then I "feather" the bangs (Okay, so I'm getting fancy now) to make it look like I didn't put a bowl on her head as I whacked away.

Once I got the bangs looking right smart, they just didn't flow well with the rest of her 'do. Inevitably, I had to cut the sides because otherwise her hair from the ears back, well, frankly, looked funny and not in sync with her newly trimmed, feathered bangs.

All of the above has taken, as I said, three days, because when I wash her hair after I cut it, I find strands that need to be cut to look like it all goes together. I have a feeling I'm still not through, but anything worthwhile is worth waiting for.

DAY 84

I think I felt the baby move.

The books say you can feel the baby as early as four months but it's not all that common. I don't remember when I first felt Courtney—because then I didn't keep a diary of daily happenings as they related to pregnancy, and because I didn't know what it was supposed to feel like.

I do remember, however, what it felt like when Courtney was six or seven months along. There was no mistaking it. And that's the kind of feeling I'm having now and at about the same spot in my abdomen.

The weight gain, as I mentioned earlier, which by the way is at three pounds over my starting weight (I lost a pound), is one of the first tangible pieces of evidence of pregnancy—besides the morning sickness, of course. The next big sign is feeling the baby as he/she is moving inside the womb.

It's a little early to *see* the movement, though. And to put my hand over the spot and feel it externally. Bryan and I spent many tender moments during my first pregnancy feeling Courtney move inside me.

We look forward to more tender moments this time around—only this time it'll be more precious, as Courtney will be able to share them, too.

DAY 85

I broke 100 for the second time yesterday.

That is, in golf. I've been playing every now and then when funds (it's a rich pregnant woman's sport) allowed since I was eight months pregnant with Courtney. Then I shot an extremely tainted fifty-two on nine at a municipal course in Virginia Beach. That's about all our funds allowed. "Very tainted," by the way, in golf terms means, among other things, heavy usage of the "toe wedge." Jack, Curtis, and Nick don't carry toe wedges in their PGA bags because if they used them, it would translate into heavy penalties.

At the time my point was, "Hey, I'm spending all our funds on golf and I'm going to play the way I want to play, have fun doing so, and come back with a respectable score for a pregnant woman in her eighth month."

Besides, at eight months it was easier to kick the ball out of the rough and onto the fairway than bend over and toss it there.

DAY 86

Bryan and I have been working hard this weekend getting the house in "show shape." I don't know if that's part of real estate lingo or not; it sounds good, though.

What's entailed here goes far beyond vacuuming—cleaning chandeliers, for example. It's amazing how much brighter a room becomes once dust, four inches thick, is removed from the bulbs. And then there's removing hard-water stains from the toilets. We have three of them (toilets, not hard-water stains). Yes, we're a three-toilet family, the envy of the neighborhood. But there's a hefty price for all this envy; these stains are quite stubborn. We'll just have to keep the lid down in the guest bathroom when we show it. We probably should keep it down anyway. I wonder what Miss Manners would have to say about toilet lid etiquette. (It's probably not good etiquette to even talk about toilet lids.)

The biggest job of the big jobs we have before us is organizing our closets to make it look like we have tons of closet space, which we don't, and that's one reason we're moving. And that poses a problem for me as I ready myself for maternity wear. My current wardrobe of maternity clothes lies wadded up in a Glad or Hefty garbage bag (I forget the brand; I probably had a coupon for it that day) that sits on my closet floor. I'm not through with my oversized, elastic, nonpregnant clothes yet, but I need to dig out the maternity stuff and hang them up, too. That will really make my closet look cramped. It should: it will be cramped.

This will not be easy to explain to potential buyers.

DAY 87

I haven't mentioned pimples in a while.

It's probably better that I haven't. If you're keeping score,

I had that one annoying pimple under my nostril that arrived in the room five minutes before I did. That pimple eventually went by the wayside. All this occurred a month or two ago.

Now I'm sporting five pimples: two on my chin, one next to my right eyebrow, and two on my forehead (thankfully, under my bangs). I feel like I should be worrying whether that cute guy who sits in the second row in algebra class will notice my pizza-like complexion, and if so, whether he'll overlook it all and discover I'm a good-hearted person worth asking out on a date nevertheless.

Actually the cute guy I did marry and I discuss pimples with unabashed candor. Further, we often get into deep conversations about all sorts of bodily shortcomings and functions. After all, he's seen me give birth.

I'm not sure that cute guy in algebra class would still ask me out after watching me give birth.

DAY 88

I had my monthly check-up today.

It's become a family activity, as Bryan leaves work, Courtney leaves her toys, and I leave—well, I don't know what I leave—to listen to the baby's heartbeat, watch the doc measure my uterus, and ask him any pressing questions about my pregnancy. The visits are certainly a lot of fun—that's because I don't have to endure the internal exams.

Courtney might have an idea of what's going on. Then again, she might not. She certainly is curious, though. While I lay on the table stripped from the belly down, Bryan holds Courtney in his lap and we discuss why we're there in the first place. Suddenly, Courtney's eyes are drawn to the medicine cabinet, from where she grabs a tube of KY Jelly and yells, "Toothpaste!"

DAY 89

I was a bit disappointed after my visit to the OB/GYN.

I asked him about feeling the baby move inside me. He said it was possible, though not probable, that I felt the baby. He reduced the odds even further when I pointed in the general area where I felt the baby. He said that couldn't be the baby. It had to be something else, he said.

Gas.

That was certainly embarrassing for two reasons. Number one, I was thinking I could at this stage feel the baby way up higher than where my uterus had grown, like around my belly-button area. So according to my reasoning, the baby was inside my spleen or liver or one of those weird organs.

Second, it was embarrassing because gas is an embarrassing subject.

Or at least it should be.

DAY 90

Sometimes it takes a major disaster to get me to put things in their proper perspective.

Hurricane Andrew—at this writing it's been downgraded to a tropical storm—has done billions of dollars' worth of damage and killed people in the Bahamas, Florida, and is still pounding southern Louisiana. News reports claim it's the costliest hurricane in U.S. history. I've been following developments closely—but probably not as closely as if I were one of the ones in Andrew's destructive path.

That's where the perspective comes in.

I spend my days worrying about gaining weight, having pimples, and wearing elastic waistbands. An event like this makes you wonder how many other pregnant women were once thinking about things like that until danger headed their way. Danger in such proportions that it included home destruction to loss of life. All of a sudden, elastic doesn't seem quite so bad.

Fourth Month

DAY 91

Now I'm officially showing.

Not that anything looks much different when people look at me, but there's one event that makes me look at pregnancy in a whole new way.

That's when you dig out the bagged-up maternity clothes, wash them, and perhaps iron them.

Nah.

Still, there comes a time in every pregnant woman's life when she has to organize her maternity wardrobe and have it ready for when that last zipper won't zip or that last button just won't button on her regular clothes. And that time has arrived for me.

I believe I have about a month's worth of zipping and

buttoning still ahead of me, but with Bryan and I getting the house ready to put on the market, my closet needs to look its best—which means "no garbage bags filled with maternity clothes lying on the floor to indicate clutter and therefore a closet that's too small and therefore a house that just doesn't provide enough storage space and therefore it's simply not suitable for any other human being on the face of this planet."

The implications go even deeper. If we can't sell our house in a reasonable length of time, four days maybe, then we're contributing to the evidence that says our country is in a recession. In turn, that hurts consumer confidence beyond the real estate market. People would simply stop buying. Our country would further sink into the depths of a depression. From there, who knows what would happen.

So it's plain to see I need to get my maternity clothes ready, for the betterment of my country.

DAY 92

In a few hours we'll be on our way to vacation.

Well, sorta.

First, we have to drop Courtney off at her grandparents' house in Spartanburg and then spend the weekend with them because our reservations don't start until Monday. But Bryan wants to get an early start. I don't blame him, I guess. When I was working full-time, I couldn't wait to get out of town when the occasion arose. Now that I've been home for more than a year, I'd rather take my time and leave whenever I feel like it. I'd just as well spend the weekend here even though it's not a great place to spend a vacation, but I don't consider my vacation to have started until we are on direct course toward Myrtle Beach.

It would be nice to take Courtney, my favorite two-year-old in the whole wide world, with us to the beach…for a day, okay, maybe a day and a half. But I know that she would rather spend the week getting totally spoiled by her grandparents. And that's what her grandparents—especially her grandmother— would rather Courtney do, too. In fact, her grandmother is taking *vacation* time to watch Courtney for us.

And she's not leaving town, either.

DAY 93

As I sit on our oceanfront balcony with the gentle South Carolina breeze cooling my slightly tinged sunburn, I feel inspired to write something creative.

But I'll have to settle for this.

Below me is a family of four with young children splashing in the pool. The boy, I guess, is a few months younger than Courtney. His sister's about three. I can figure out who their parents are without knowing who their parents are because here they are at Myrtle Beach...with NO TAN!

There's also Byron and Christy, a couple on their honeymoon, who also don't have tans—but I don't think it's because of toddlers.

Meanwhile, back in Spartanburg, Courtney is probably having the time of her life with her grandparents while Bryan and I are getting tans that'll make us the envy of everyone back in Roanoke. Imagine, we'll have great tans on top of having three toilets in our house!

The careful observer would have no trouble telling that we—tanned or not—have at least one young child. That's because we spend a lot of our time comparing all these other kids to Courtney.

But we do all this comparing while working on our tans.

DAY 94

I like this beach.

There are so many fat women here that I'm convinced there must be some kind of convention going on. Bryan doesn't think so because he says they don't seem to know each other.

Nevertheless, I feel better knowing there's an influx of fat women on this beach. I'd say only 2.3 percent of the women on the strip today still possess that enviable vertical "ditch" down their abdomens. But it's hard to see them because of all the fat women.

Bryan assures me he doesn't look at other women. I don't look at other women, either. But when you feel like you're carrying a partially inflated balloon in your tummy, a sense of insecurity can set in.

Although for the past three and a half months it has sounded as though I've been equating fat with pregnancy, I certainly don't mean to. Bryan's always telling me how beautiful I am when I'm pregnant.

That's because *he's* not pregnant.

DAY 95

Want big lips?

I've unlocked the secret to having lips so big they eclipse the sun. Here's what you do: go out on the beach at the peak of the day without sunscreen or suntan lotion and get a sunburn. Naturally, your lips will get parched in the process.

At this point, your lips aren't really swollen, though they may feel as if they are. Kind of like being pregnant. Anyway, at bedtime, apply generous amounts of Vaseline or your petroleum product of choice on your lips and settle down for a good night's sleep.

The next morning, you'll awake feeling your face is heavier than usual. Perhaps your husband awakens you with a loud scream as he looks with horror at your swollen lips. After all, it is a grotesque sight: lips turned practically inside out and dangling below your chin. You wonder how you'll brush your teeth without drooling all over the sink. Again, another grotesque sight.

And that's the skin care tip of the day.

DAY 96

Today I'd like to talk about the exploitation of pregnant women.

It's all around us. Unless you're pregnant you probably don't notice or are immune to this impropriety. Like sex, violence, Monistat-7 commercials, and cuss words on TV. Where are all the gasps today when TBS airs *Gone with the*

Wind and Clark Gable tells Vivien Leigh he doesn't really care. (This is a family book so I will not repeat verbatim what he said fifty-some-odd years ago, but if you are old enough to go to a PG movie unsupervised, then you know what Clark told Vivien, so I don't have to repeat it here.) Besides, they didn't cuss during the Civil War; cussing began sometime during the Wilson Administration.

But back to the pregnancy exploitation. The other evening, Bryan and I were walking along the strip back to our motel after a roaring night of playing Ms. Pacman and sharing a snowcone. We're on a budget; otherwise we would've splurged for *two* snowcones. Suddenly, a very pregnant woman—she must've been in her eleventh or twelfth month—appears out of a parking lot and says she'd like to ask us a few questions.

You just can't be rude to a pregnant woman. It's un-American. So we let her ask us questions. Not surprisingly, her four questions focused on religion, and after we unrudely answered them, two other people—for whom we may have not stopped to answer questions to begin with, and if we did, we might have been rude about it—emerged to sell us on their religion. I should mention these folks were *not* pregnant.

It's obvious that a very pregnant woman was being used here, as noted by this soon-to-be-very-pregnant woman.

DAY 97

You try to plan for everything, and still you come home after a long vacation to a mysterious odor lurking in your kitchen.

Sound like an intro to a bad commercial? Nope. This is reality. It's been nearly twenty hours, and I still haven't discovered what's creating an awful smell in my kitchen.

I take that back. The smell was much worse when we first came home, and I found one culprit immediately: a half-pound of opened hamburger meat dating back to ancient Babylon. A few squirts of air freshener, and I thought that would be the end of that—of course, after I threw away the meat.

I was proud of myself before we left town. I thoroughly—well, almost—cleaned out the fridge, tossing things like milk and other short-lived dairy products that would stink up the place upon our return. I just forgot to look in the meat compartment, that's all. I'm pretty sure it's not the kitchen trash can. I'd like to think I wouldn't be stupid enough to let the above-mentioned food items rot at room temperature in my kitchen. Who knows what could happen? Gangrene, maybe.

So now there's one offensive smell and hopefully just one offensive cause of this smell. Actually, I have tracked it down to the freezer. Popsicles? Ice cubes? TV dinners? I do have some *chicken* freezing away in there, but I've isolated the chicken from the rest of the freezer inhabitants, and I'm not convinced that's the culprit.

Bryan hasn't complained about it. Of course, I should mention he left within ten hours of returning home on a business trip to Toledo. Is that a coincidence or what? Courtney hasn't complained, either. Of course, if you've seen some of her dirty diapers that should be banned in thirty-one states and yet never bother her, then you'd understand why an unpleasant kitchen odor wouldn't faze her.

Maybe it's hormones. Maybe being pregnant, I'm smelling things that just aren't there.

The mystery continues.

DAY 98

Before I move on with today's thought, I'd like to say I think I've solved the odor problem in my kitchen. I say "think" because I've had a stuffy nose since returning from vacation (I think I inhaled too many sea oats), and I'm not positive the offensive smell lurking in my kitchen, specifically near the fridge, has been eradicated. It seems I sensed correctly. It was indeed the chicken in the freezer.

Anyway, as I sit here watching Chang and Edberg battle it out in the fifth set in semi-final action of the U.S. Open, I'm reminded that it's about time I start to watch my bellybutton. Perhaps that sounds strange, or maybe I need to get out more. But the fact of the matter is that my girth continues to grow and so, following the theory of relativity, my bellybutton will disappear soon. At least that's what happened to some of my relatives.

My appetite is up, which is definitely something that hastens the disappearance of the bellybutton. Naturally, I'm talking about "innies." I don't know about "outies." During pregnancy, the innie turns into an outie. Actually, now that I'm thinking about it, an innie technically shouldn't be called a bellybutton to begin with. It's more like a bellyhole. An outie is a true bellybutton.

These pregnancy hormones surely cause you to think weird thoughts.

DAY 99

Pete Sampras has diarrhea.

Pete's in the finals of the U.S. Open today, and after winning the semis yesterday, he fled from the court immediately after winning match point and headed for the nearest bathroom. A flood of reporters and camera people darted after him.

Poor pitiful Pete.

Yesterday, the CBS correspondent reported that officials said Pete had "stomach cramps." That's certainly a bit more tactful than the way they described it today. Then they go on to talk about the rest of Pete's day yesterday, what he ate, how much sleep he got, etc.

I'm embarrassed for the poor guy. It's one thing for me to write about my own bodily functions—in my case morning sickness, which I hope is long gone. It's another for someone else to talk about it.

I guess it's a sports thing. Another sports thing I've always been appalled at is how announcers casually reveal players' age, height, and (gasp) weight. I have a problem with that. For one thing, the players usually can't defend themselves when the statement is made. That's because they're on the field playing. That's what players do.

If it were me, and they flashed some fancy, state-of-the-art computer graphics on the TV screen that told the world I was thirty years old, five feet six inches, and 130 pounds. I'd let it be known that they weighed me right after I had meatloaf for dinner and didn't get a chance to take off my shoes. So I really weighed 124 pounds. (It was good meatloaf.)

Now that I'm more than four months along, I've resolved not to let weight get me down—because it's constantly going up.

Shoes or not.

DAY 100

One thing the vacation did for me is to get me back on track with my walking routine. I confess I slacked off a bit—okay, a lot—and began to feel a certain flabbiness that I couldn't blame on pregnancy. Well, I could blame it on pregnancy, but deep down inside all that flab I knew it was laziness.

Tennis is over for the season—of course, singles has been long over. Golf is so cost-prohibitive that it's a rare sporting event for us. And there are just a few games left for our softball team. So I need to rely on walking to get the exercise I need for both my body and my mind. I'm lucky; Bryan comes home from work and watches Courtney for thirty minutes or so while I take my walk. I'm in a better mood for having done so, and I know my growing body and the body that's growing inside me are profiting from the exercise, as well.

That's what is important now.

DAY 101

I received something interesting in the mail yesterday.

The first line reads, "World's Most Sensational Doll!" What else could that be but the Mother-With-Baby doll? No, they didn't send me the doll, but rather a coupon allowing me to purchase this thing for $10. The only aspect of this ad I liked was the fact that they didn't price it at $9.99 to make folks think it was a whole lot cheaper than $10.

On the back of this ad, I discover this mother doll's name is Karen. Coincidence? It comes with two extra maternity out-fits, pocketbook (even I don't have a maternity pocketbook), comb and brush for mommy (those are personal hygiene items mommy should have whether she's pregnant or not), blanket, towel (for the big water break, I guess), two hangers (for the spiffy maternity outfits obviously), barrette, rattle, hand mirror, and diaper for the baby.

The purpose of this doll, it goes on to explain, is to teach children the miracle of birth. I agree. The birth of a baby is a miracle. However, this doll is supposed to be a "warm and wonderful *educational* experience for your child" (emphasis added). Let's talk female anatomy for a second. This baby is in "mommy's *tummy*," (emphasis added again), according to the ad. Someone gave these ad writers a bum steer. Probably male writers anyway. Then, this Karen Mother's pregnant tummy becomes *flat* again after the baby is born.

Yeah, right.

At the bottom of this ad are three photos showing how the birthing process works. In essence, the baby emerges from the mommy's tummy in the same fashion as the alien did in the movie by the same name. Not as scary, though. Then the baby pops out of a big oval cut in the mommy's tummy that will prohibit her from wearing a two-piece swimsuit again.

That's a shame, too, seeing how flat her postpartum tummy becomes.

DAY 102

One of the best ways to prepare yourself for childbirth is to watch those animal shows on TV. The Discovery Channel and PBS are full of them, and they're a must-see for pregnant women.

Today's episode on *Profiles in Nature* focuses on the Canada goose. What immediately bothers me is that it's not the *Canadian* goose, which to me seems to be more grammatically correct. But I'm not the one naming the animals here.

Something that interests me is that the gander hangs around with his spouse as she gives birth, lays eggs or whatever, and protects his family from muskrats, foxes, and Monistat-7 commercials. The female Canada goose lays five to six eggs at a time. And do these quintuplets and sextuplets ever make the cover of *McCall's*? Imagine having to come up with that many names. Bryan and I can't even decide on one. (Then again, the geese don't have to try to find names to go with "Nutt.")

Now they show two children about seven or eight years old reaching under this mother goose and taking one of her newly hatched offspring, and she doesn't seem to mind. Yeah, right. I now dip into my memory bank and recall my feelings toward my firstborn shortly after birth...I certainly wouldn't allow a second-grader to take her away from me.

The difference is the goose was *sitting* on her little one. I'd certainly want someone to relieve me from that discomfort.

DAY 103

It's official. We're selling our house.

This is the first time we've sold anything bigger than a tennis racket. We are going the FISBO route—that is, For Sale By Owner—for a month. Bryan's already committed to newspaper ads for that period of time. I bought FISBO signs this morning at Wal-Mart. And I've previously written grammatically correct information sheets on our house and worked up ads for community bulletin boards.

We're set.

Of course, we're not sure what to do if someone actually wants to buy our house. I leave that stuff up to my engineer-husband, who's got a master's degree. My job is just to get them here. If we can't sell it on our own, then we'll swallow our pride and forget about all the big bucks we could've saved and get a realtor.

The beauty of it all is that we don't have to sell our house to begin with. Rates are down, and the rate we have on our house stinks, and we'd like to have a house with all the living space on one level, and we see this as a type of refinancing.

The scary thing, however, is that we may get caught between houses by the time the baby's born. And that would definitely create havoc with the "nesting syndrome" that'll occur within me a few weeks before delivery.

We'd better get a move on then.

DAY 104

Courtney's sick today.

And there's nothing more pathetic than a sick child. Well, with the exception of the attempted comeback of the Brady Bunch when Greg and the gang were all grown up—remember? Marcia was an alcoholic, Bobby was a race car driver who got in a bad wreck, and Cindy was a disc jockey. The actress who played Jan in the original series had the good sense not to sign up for that one. (Actually, I don't think many people noticed there was a new Jan.)

I got off track. Anyway, it's been a while since Courtney has been sick with congestion and a deep cough. Typically, it takes her a while to get over it, too. After church, I bought her some medicine, and right now she's taking a nap. Bryan is too. He's sick, but it involves his stomach. I won't go into detail.

All I can say about myself today is that I've gained nine pounds—not in one day, however, but since the beginning of my pregnancy. I don't remember being sick during my first pregnancy, with the exception of morning sickness. I was lucky and enjoyed a healthy nine months for the most part.

I hope I'm just as lucky this time.

DAY 105

I'm back on the pill.

The horse pill, that is. During the peak of morning sickness, I was advised by my doctor to shelve the vitamin pills because they aggravated my stomach. A lot of things aggravate my stomach: jeans with tight waistlines, for example. Or if you called my stomach names, such as pudgy, chubby, or even fat. My stomach would get aggravated by that.

I've heard that it's the vitamin pills taken during pregnancy that cause babies to be so big nowadays. Back when I was born, it was rare to have eight-pound babies. Now eight-pounders are quite common. People don't blink twice at ten-pounders, either. The woman having the ten-pounder certainly does, though.

Courtney was eight pounds, twelve ounces. Courtney was a C-baby, mainly because of the size of her head, which was indirectly related to her weight. My doctor isn't scalpel-happy, but he says he can tell if I'll need another Caesarean by the eighth month. So there's not much point in me worrying about it until then.

So right now, I'll simply worry about whether the vitamins will make this baby's head too big, which will mean I'll need another C-section.

DAY 106

I had an uneventful OB/GYN visit today.

Well, it was eventful for Courtney, who heard the baby's heartbeat for the first time. Bryan and I got to hear it a month ago through the stethoscope—try putting a stethoscope on a two-year-old and expect her to hear something out of it. This time the doctor put one of those things on my stomach that allows the sound to be amplified throughout the examining room. Sort of like a miniature PA system.

The baby's heartbeat was very fast—at least it seemed fast to us. The doctor says that's normal. I've gained the proper amount of weight, and my uterus is growing normally. All of this I'm thankful for.

No news is good news.

DAY 107

Yesterday marked the end of two things: playing softball and selling our house.

After getting plowed over by a 197-pound guy at second base last week and getting plowed in the nose by a one-and-a-half-pound softball last night, and in view of the fact that we rarely win (our team's two wins this season came when we were at the beach; maybe that should tell us something), I'm retiring my jersey. Last week's close encounter could have been devastating for me and especially my baby, but thankfully it wasn't. Last night's encounter had nothing to do with being pregnant, just being in the line of a hard-hit ball to left field and my glove not anticipating the first bad hop...smack dab in my face.

Our decision to take the house off the market after three days was a bit less dramatic. Kind of boring, actually. After looking at other houses in our price range, we decided they weren't of the same caliber as ours. It simply isn't worth the closing costs to move again, although taking advantage of the nifty rates made it tempting. But not tempting enough.

Besides, our For Sale sign blew down during a storm yesterday afternoon, and it was easier not to put it back up.

DAY 107

It's broken.

That's right. It's not too often you find a thirty-year-old pregnant woman—nearly five months along—with a broken nose due to an unfortunate bad bounce. That bad bounce, to refresh your memory, occurred from a line-drive to left field, and I happened to be in the line of fire.

What happens next is up in the air. In four days, the doctor will determine if my nose needs to be "manipulated"—I prefer the term "shoved"—back into its original position. This manipulation, to keep this discussion in medical terms, must take place no later than seven days from the time the injury took place. In four days it will be Day Six. Sounds like a hostage situation.

Determining whether this manipulation must occur is dependent on two factors: how crooked my nose is as a result of the natural setting over the next six days, and perhaps more importantly, at least from a respiratory point of view, how well I can breathe. Since one side of my nose tends to be leaning toward the other side, this is probably the more pressing issue at stake.

However, this manipulation must be performed with local anesthesia only—no funky drugs allowed because I'm pregnant, and I've learned to Just Say No. The doctor says that the procedure may be more painful because of that.

Of course, it may be more painful if I can't breathe.

DAY 108

It's funny. You buy, and especially allow your child's grandparents to buy, your child all sorts of toys—from puzzles, to dollhouses, to stuffed animals, to riding vehicles, to just about everything Sesame Street peddles—and your child ends up playing with your $365.95 Casio keyboard.

And she plays it better than you do.

I'm not too bad. In my nonpregnant days, I learned the scales and could find middle C with virtually no problem—unless I couldn't find my instruction manual. I remembered "All Cows Eat Grass" for the A, C, E, and G chords from my eighth grade music class. And I remembered "All Good Boys Do Fine" for the same corresponding chords. Of course, I didn't know much about how to apply these catchy sentences into a musical work of art. Or even how they applied to "Frère Jacques."

Since then, I had learned to play a few tunes, some with a chord accompaniment, but even that stretched my musical talents to the limit. Now Courtney seems to have a solid interest in music, unlike Mom and Dad, and the propensity to be mighty good at it.

That's obviously the result of my playing Janet Jackson's "Rhythm Nation" while in labor during Courtney's birth.

DAY 109

Today we bought a new mattress and box springs for what will be Courtney's bed in a few weeks.

From what I'm told, it's important to get the firstborn out of the crib way before the second born barges in. I think there's something psychological about it in the firstborn's mind, like "in with the new, out with the old." Or "throwing out the baby with the bath water." Of course, I don't know how these psychologists *know* what goes on in the mind of a two-year-old, but there's no need to risk it. Courtney's going to need a bed anyhow in time. So we ordered it, and it should arrive in two to three weeks.

And the baby's not due to arrive for another four months, so that should give us plenty of time to acclimate Courtney to her new room and new bed.

However, our guests will find no room in the inn when they come to visit us from that point on. Actually, we'll give up our room and sleep on our huge comfortable sofa downstairs when folks get an urge to spend the night at our house. We're hospitable people.

Let's just hope the new surroundings will be quite agreeable to Courtney.

DAY 110

I'd like to add another one to the "Movies Not To See When You're Pregnant" list: *The Hand that Rocks the Cradle*.

The list I came up with earlier in this pregnancy mainly included movies that were gross and not recommended for pregnant women sensitive to morning sickness. There are a few nasty scenes in this flick, but not bad enough to make the earlier list.

We rented *The Hand that Rocks the Cradle* knowing full well it wouldn't be an instructional movie for parents illustrating new and improved methods to get your infant to sleep at night. Rather, it's a testament to why moms should stay home with their kids—until the kids are twenty-eight-and-a-half.

Actually, the mom in this movie *did* stay home, but she felt she needed a nanny anyway because she wanted to build a greenhouse in her backyard. Well, a three-month-old cramps your style when you try to build a greenhouse, so you have to have a nanny. But the nanny is this young and beautiful widow of the mom's OB/GYN who committed suicide after the mom accused him of sexually molesting her during an exam while she was pregnant. Only the mom doesn't know who the nanny really is—it would've been a lot simpler if she hired someone like Aunt Clara on *Bewitched*.

Somebody should have checked references here.

DAY 111

I really don't like dwelling on this weight thing, especially after I practically vowed to stop dwelling on it.

I've been pretty proud of myself for giving in to the fact that I'm gaining weight. That's a normal, healthy part of having a baby, and I've accepted that. I've accepted the fact that I've gained nine pounds, and it goes without saying that I'm in the non-figure-flattering-elastic-maternity-pants stage now. And I've done all this without murmuring.

Well, not excessive murmuring, perhaps.

But today, they're pressing my good nature. I go to the nose doctor to see if he has to "manipulate" my broken nose back into (or *beak* into) place. He doesn't, and that's fine because the whole thing sounds gross anyway. What's highly annoying to this pregnant woman nearly five months along is that they had to weigh me so the nose doctor could make that decision. And take my blood pressure, too, but that's not nearly as irritating as finding out I'm three pounds heavier than six days ago when I went in for my monthly OB/GYN checkup. Three pounds!

What's so unprofessional is that both the nose department and OB/GYN department are in the *same clinic*. You'd think they'd synchronize their scales or something to avoid such highly annoying situations.

That's certainly the last time I'll break my nose while I'm pregnant.

DAY 112

I'm beginning to repeat the patterns of my first pregnancy.

I thought some of these patterns, however, occurred in later months, not where I am now. But because I didn't keep a diary of what I was doing when, I really don't know for the sure, and I guess the months just run together.

Nevertheless, I'm eating oatmeal, which is something I eat even when I'm not pregnant, just not with the same frequency as I've been eating it lately. And it seems the best time to eat oatmeal is about two or three hours after dinner. Last night, I was craving a bowl, but the saucepan was crusted over from the previous night's bowl, and I hadn't run the dishwasher yet.

So I merely settled for Raisin Bran.

The other pattern I've picked up again is sleeping with a sofa pillow. I still sleep with my husband, but he's not as easy to prop under my tummy.

DAY 113

I've got to quit reading.

At least, quit reading controversial stuff about birthing babies. I'd prefer to be in Miss Prissy's camp and proclaim that I don't know nothing about birthing no babies. Actually, I'd probably use better grammar to make such a proclamation.

The article I read had to do with the evolution of the birthing process in this country, with undertones about how it may be better to go the midwife route than the traditional OB/GYN route. The article made me nervous; I don't know any midwives.

I guess one point in the article struck close to home, or rather to my tummy: the overuse of C-sections. I feel confident my doctor had to do a "C" on me, due to Courtney's head—and her body in general—being too big to fit through the...I don't know what part she didn't fit through; she just didn't fit through. I had been in labor for nine hours by that time. I wasn't in the mood for a detailed lesson on the ins and outs of the birth process. Actually, I should have been boning up on the subject the preceding nine months. Come to think of it, I did; I just wasn't in the mood for a pop quiz.

And in a way, that's what the article was saying—that too many doctors say the C-word without giving an explanation, and the patients merely accept their word for it. The doctors' advantage: more money for them and for the hospital since the stay ends up being twice as long. Kind of like when you go to the drive-through window at a fast food place, and you order a cheeseburger, and the cashier asks you if you want cole slaw to go with that, and you say no, thinking cole slaw would be gross with a cheeseburger, and because there's a lot of static on those speakers the cashier assumes you want cole slaw because he thinks cole slaw is just the thing you need to top off your meal, and then you pay for it, and you don't notice you

.

even got the cole slaw until you get home, and it's too much trouble to take it back and get a fifty-nine-cent refund because the gas would cost you more than that, so you just accept the situation.

The difference with a C-section is that it costs more than fifty-nine cents and you don't have to wait until you get home to find out you got it.

DAY 114

C-sections really don't scare me…mainly because I know what to expect. Odds are I can expect to have another one in four and a half months.

Vaginal births do scare me, though…mainly because I don't know what to expect. The thought of a baby barreling through a tiny opening, causing rips and tears—if not an incision—is as scary to moms who've undergone C-sections as the thought of having the baby pulled out through the abdominal wall is to moms who've undergone vaginal births.

It all boils down to what you're familiar with.

DAY 115

I received my monthly baby-on-the-way newsletter from my hospital today. It set me back just a bit; it's for those in their *sixth* month.

No. That can't be right. I can't be that far along yet. I guess I should contact the editors of the newsletter; they'd want to know they're sending me information I can't use for another six weeks or so.

Being in the sixth month sounds so scary. It's like birth is just around the corner, in three months or so. I haven't even gotten Courtney out of diapers yet, much less out of the crib and into a regular bed to make room for baby. I haven't gotten out the infant clothes from storage. I haven't picked out appropriate birth announcements, much less even gotten a catalog to order them. I haven't bought the baby's going-home-from-the-hospital outfit yet. I haven't bought any newborn diapers or any formula.

I haven't started my Christmas shopping yet. I haven't even bought Halloween candy or thawed out the Thanksgiving turkey—of course, I haven't bought that either.

And I'm just now starting to panic.

DAY 116

Ah, the privilege of the pregnant.

Today, I received the privilege of being first in line at lunch at a church-related ladies' retreat just because I'm pregnant. Another woman was pregnant, too, due two months after I am and still in the unfortunate stage of morning sickness. I think she enjoyed being at the head of the line, as well, in spite of her morning sickness.

It's a gorgeous autumn day at this camp in the Blue Ridge Mountains. The clear azure sky combines with leaves just turning their golden tones for a scene only God could create. It's a day such as this that makes me pause and reflect on all God has given me: a loving husband, a beautiful daughter, and a baby on the way for starters. It's a day that makes me forget about my weight gain and remember that I've been blessed beyond measure.

And that's a privilege of the pregnant *and* nonpregnant.

DAY 117

My wardrobe is shrinking.

I must have stood hopelessly in front of my closet for fifteen minutes this morning to pick out a nonmaternity outfit to wear to church. I finally found one, complete with an elastic waistband and a bulky sweater to cover that fact. Actually, I received a few compliments from some kind sisters in the church who know what it's like to be in my current stage of pregnancy.

Sort of like no-man's—or no-woman's—land. There's no mistaking, even to the untrained eye, that you're bigger. But pregnant? Casual observers may think not, which tempts you to bite the bullet and plunge your body into huge sweatshirts that read "Baby on Board."

But I like my nonpregnant clothes and wish to wear them until the seams can't take it any more. Of course, my girth hasn't been able to squeeze into a nonmaternity pair of pants in weeks, but there's still a shimmering glow of hope for the oversized dresses and skirts hanging in my closet. Except for the outfit I wore this morning, these outfits are those I don't normally like to wear because they make me look chunky because they're bigger than I am. Now that I'm in a pinch, or rather that my body's in a pinch when I try to get into my other clothes, these misfit outfits are the most fashionable things I own.

At least for the next couple of weeks or so.

DAY 118

Today is one of those days, when I have to realize I can't do everything I used to…at least not all in one day.

I'm exhausted, and the day's just half over. I grocery-shopped, worked-out, and cleaned-up part of the house. Maybe it's the hyphenated chores that are wearing me out.

I did have a good workout, although sometimes I feel like I'm fighting an uphill battle because I know another fifteen or twenty pounds of weight gain is on the horizon, making my horizon that much wider. But I must look beyond the physical weight and consider that I'll be in much better shape to take on labor and birth—especially if a C-section becomes necessary—if I keep up the workouts during pregnancy. Plus, I'll feel better in general, not lazy and depressed, so it's good for my mental health, as well. Whew, adding all those commas to that sentence wears me out, too, after a day like today.

But I feel better knowing I'm grammatically correct.

DAY 119

That newsletter I received a few days ago outlines why I gain what I gain. Here's the breakdown (based on a twenty-five-pound weight gain):
- Baby: seven pounds
- Placenta: one and a half pounds

• Amniotic Fluid: one and a half pounds (I always get amniotic fluid mixed up with the placenta. And it's no wonder; they weigh the same.)

• Uterine Enlargement: one and three-quarter pounds

• Breast Tissue: one pound (or six cup sizes at least)

• Increase in Blood Volume: two and a half pounds

• Retained Fluids: three pounds (the number-one female excuse for weight gain. By the way, I usually retain eleven to thirteen pounds in fluid when I'm pregnant, and when I'm not.)

• Stored Body Fat: seven pounds (Rice Krispie Treats, vanilla milkshakes, cinnamon rolls, etc.)

DAY 120

It's no wonder pregnant women gain so much, especially if they follow physician guidelines for eating healthy. Let's consider a few daily recommendations.

Eight ounces of lean meat, fish, chicken, or turkey and at least once a week add a glandular meat. I don't know any glandular meats. I know some glands, like the pituitary gland, but I don't think I want to eat one of those.

An egg. Some docs say only four or five a week, however, because of the cholesterol.

Four eight-ounce cups of milk. That's a lot of milk.

One ounce of cheese. I can handle that.

Two cupfuls of fresh, green, leafy, raw vegetables and other colored vegetables each day. Stuff like lettuce, tomatoes, cucumbers, celery, and others, to give you the urge to say "What's up, Doc?" at the next OB/GYN visit.

Eight ounces of cooked vegetables, such as asparagus (have you checked the price of asparagus lately?), beans, broccoli, peas, spinach, carrots, brussel sprouts, or turnips. Something about iron.

One serving of whole wheat, rice, or grain cereals. I wonder where Fruit Loops fit in?

Fifth Month

DAY 121

If this baby grows up to become an airline pilot, earn a living as a travel agent, or drive a Greyhound bus, I'll know why.

That's because this baby's done a lot of traveling in the first five months of life without ever leaving the womb. Very economical on his/her part. Not necessarily on mom's.

His/her travels from the womb are sort of like The Shopping Channel. You know, shop 'til you drop in the comfort and convenience of your living room. The womb, from what I understand (certainly not from what I remember), is the fetus's living room.

From Baton Rouge, Louisiana to Richmond, Virginia, I figured I've traveled most of the southeast by car this summer and fall, totaling thousands of miles—and thousands of trips to roadside bathrooms.

While most of our travels have been for pleasure, today's is for business, as I'm helping this baby's grandmother work a spectacular craft show in a cotton-pickin' town of Canton, Mississippi, not too far from Jerry Clower's hometown of Yazoo City.

DAY 122

Here's a gift idea for that man on your list who's expecting a child soon.

I don't know what it's called. Somebody was telling me about it the other day and said that Donahue wore it during one of his shows. And everybody knows what a fashion-plate Phil is.

Anyway, it's a pregnancy simulator for men to wear to discover what it feels like to be pregnant. From what I understand, it's much more than a thirty-pound weight that hangs around the abdomen. No. The weight, while most of it is centered there, is dispersed like it is on a pregnant woman's body. Further, the apparatus even makes the wearer go to the bathroom more often.

Bryan said he wouldn't mind wearing something like that.

I would. He had enough empathy pains during the morning sickness stage as it was, so I'd hate to hear him complain about the "real" thing.

DAY 123

The pregnancy hormones went haywire again today.

I know this because I wouldn't have done what I did today had I not had strange hormones causing me to do what I did. Confession cleans the soul—or something like that—so it's best to do some self-cleaning: I chased Goober around a crowded mall for two hours.

Gasp.

In retrospect, I'm sincerely ashamed because there was so much more I could have done with those two hours than hunt down a goofy fictional character from *The Andy Griffith Show*, and on top of that, I never did find him. My purpose for this stupid antic? To get him to autograph a Mayberry trivia book I bought for Bryan for Christmas.

I was misled. The day before, I called this brand-new mall— well, it's more like a flea market—that was slated to open with all sorts of hoopla, including an *all-day* appearance by Goober—or so I was told. I called a friend—at least I hope she's still my friend—to accompany me to this grand opening and help me get Goober's autograph. We even paid fifty cents each to get into this mall, a place I wouldn't go back to even if it were free because they told me he'd be there all day, and he wasn't. Rather, it seems he stayed a mere two hours and was mighty difficult to find while he was there. So I came back empty-autographed.

I wasted all that time trying to get Goober's autograph, which I never received. It's got to be these crazy hormones, causing a rare case of FGS—Find Goober Syndrome.

DAY 124

I think Bryan was trying to encourage me, praise me, and perhaps even compliment me, but it didn't come out that way.

At least it didn't enter my ears that way.

At a recent workout at the "Y" together, I had gotten through a grueling ten minutes on the steps and ten minutes on the bike and was in the middle of my reps on the military press, or whatever it's called. Bryan paused from his routine to watch me lift thirty pounds over my head ten times and to tell me how proud he is of me. How thoughtful.

Had he gone back to his routine and finished his workout without another word, I'd have been happier. However, he goes on to tell me how he wouldn't have the willpower and commitment to work out as often as I have if he were in my Reeboks. Knowing that I have gained a lot of weight and still have a lot of weight to gain, I am really to be admired. Knowing that no matter how much I work out, I'm still going to get bigger and bigger. Knowing that all this weight gain is out of my control, I press on nonetheless.

How discouraging.

DAY 125

In the last six days, I've spent more than thirty-five hours traveling in my Subaru across the Southeast.

It certainly shows, at least on the scales, as I'm now tipping them at an additional five pounds more than at my last doctor's visit. Let's see. That means I've put on five pounds in three weeks. I could figure out what that would be per week, but the final figure—and how it's affected my figure—is depressing enough.

DAY 126

Bryan wants to make a chart.

It's a chart that has caused a flurry of mixed reactions.

Bryan, the engineer, wants to chart my weight gain. Specifically, he wants to make a chart that compares my weight gain during this pregnancy with that of my first pregnancy. Bryan, the husband who's been working out nearly every day to get in better shape and shed a few pounds, thinks this would be neat.

I'm not so sure.

For the sake of comparison, it might be interesting. I gained thirty-six pounds with Courtney in nine months; after four months of this pregnancy, I have gained nine pounds. (Incidentally, I don't consider my all-of-a-sudden weight gain at the nose doctor official because I'm sure some of that weight could be attributed to the swelling in my nose.)

For the sake of my self-esteem during these scale-sensitive months, it might be distressing. To begin with, this chart would feature a line that goes nowhere but up. That can be distressing if I see it on paper. It's distressing enough when I see it on the scales.

The collection of scientific data may be difficult, however, because I weighed on "manual" scales before and now I weigh on "electronic" scales that calculate my pounds to the nearest tenth. It can detect whether I had an extra piece of cheesecake for dessert the night before. So, Bryan says, the chart would not show an accurate picture of my weight gain in comparison to the time before because I didn't use the same scales.

Therefore, Bryan is considering punting the entire project.

For the sake of me, it's a relief.

DAY 127

Today I enter the last month of my second trimester. (Sound of trumpets playing "Hail to the Pregnant Woman in Her Sixth Month" fills the air in the distance.)

My, time flies.

It really does. I can't remember what I did during the first two months of the second trimester. This is supposed to be the most enjoyable trimester of all, they say, because the morning sickness is usually history, and you can still see your feet. Both have held true for me, but there has to be more enjoyment to it than that.

Maybe it's during this time that I should be invited to more social events. That would certainly be enjoyable. Or how about enjoying carefree afternoons—while Bryan watched Courtney and while I caught up on my reading or sketching or just doing nothing in particular. That would be fun, too. Here's the ultimate enjoyable thing to do during the second trimester: eating out at fancy restaurants every night of the week and not having the calories or the expense count against you.

So far, our social calendar is limited. I don't know the meaning of the term "carefree afternoon," much less how to apply it to my life in the second trimester. And our idea of eating out at a fancy restaurant is the three of us sitting down to dine at the K&W Cafeteria after Sunday evening church services.

But I suppose what's enjoyable to one pregnant woman in her second trimester may not be to another. I'm thankful for the passing of morning sickness, and frankly, I enjoy seeing my feet.

DAY 128

My maternity bra is killing me.

Which reminds me. I need a new pair of maternity hose. I'm currently unable to take very big steps in my regular panty hose…baby steps, if you will. Plus, one strong gust of wind will blow my hose down to my ankles. It's time I gave in to the megahose that will support my expanded girth.

Maybe it hasn't expanded as much as I think it has. This morning at Wal-Mart, a woman about my age and with at least one child and I were discussing diaper coupons. She was envious that I had two $1-off coupons, and she knew not where to get even one. I felt sorry for her and explained they can be found in the Sunday paper and obtained from friends whose kids are already toilet-trained.

Anyway, it's not the diaper coupon dilemma that sticks with me, although it was probably the most intellectual conversation I've had all day—besides talking to Courtney about how a plastic flying bat at a supermarket Halloween display would not swoop down and attack her. I still don't think she believes me. Actually, that lady at Wal-Mart couldn't believe I'm due in February. She said, and I'm paraphrasing here, "My, you're not showing at all to be due in February."

Maybe I can wait a few more weeks on the maternity hose.

DAY 129

Fabian was a bean-grower.

I just don't know what the '50s singer's parents were thinking of when they came up with that one. You know he had to be the brunt of a lot of jokes in his class—unless he was an agriculture major.

Actually, I don't know if Fabian had any other professional interests, but I do know by extensive research—I checked out a book on names from the library today—that Fabian is derived from the Latin meaning bean-grower. Deeper reading of this book reveals that Rebecca means "snare" (another book says rebellious), Portia is a word relating to pigs (I actually know someone with that name), and Clifton means "from the farm at the cliff."

This is an old book, copyright 1943, when Ashley was a boy's name. I know at least 1,246 girls with that name who were born since 1981. Most of the names are funky, for lack of a better adjective. Here are some funky names for boys as listed on page 71: Denman (where a man lies on the couch and watches Monday Night Football), Doane (isn't that a pill for achy backs?), Dorian (meaning: A Dorian. Original, huh?), Dudley (everybody would expect him to do-right), Duff (definitely wouldn't go with Nutt), Dugald (I can imagine lots of schoolground fights over that one), Duncan (what you do to doughnuts), Dunstan (would you name your son after a brown rock?), and Durward (I thought Endora made that one up).

Maybe this book won't help in naming our baby, but it will definitely help us in what we *shouldn't* name our baby.

DAY 130

Today has been quite hectic.

I've been busy cleaning up the house for weekend company. In fact, it's worn me out so much that I broke down and asked Bryan to vacuum for me. He said, "Sure." I think he's looking forward to it after a hectic day as an engineer.

But I have to remember I don't always have the strength at my fingertips that I'm accustomed to having. And sometimes, I need a little help.

Maybe it's time to reach for the Milk of Magnesia.

DAY 131

To buy a maternity coat or not to buy a maternity coat, that is the question.

And the answer is no.

I realize I'm taking a chance, considering I'm due in mid-February. But I realize that this will be the last time I'll be pregnant, and maternity coats aren't cheap. So we're talking about an expensive, oversized coat I'll be able to wear maybe two months, assuming the weather is cold enough to require it.

But it's like whether or not you carry an umbrella with you. If you do, it won't rain. If you don't, it will. Same thing with maternity coats. I have this on reliable sources that if I don't buy one this winter, we'll definitely enter another ice age.

It's a chance I'm willing to take.

DAY 132

There's something special about Courtney.

I mean something more special than what I see that's special in my own twenty-nine-month-old daughter. In other words, I write without bias.

Today at the grocery store, Courtney was in an exceptionally fun mood, singing up and down the aisle. From the bread aisle all the way to the frozen food section, she entertained shoppers with "Old McDonald Had a Farm." You know, E..I..E..I..Ooooo. Then breaking into a medley, she sings "Jesus Loves Me." A lady near the lasagna suddenly stops her price-comparing to watch this child prodigy and gives Courtney a round of applause as she concludes—not because Courtney's finished, but because she was so good. The lady asks me how old Courtney is and marvels at her ability to fluctuate notes and pronounce words so distinctly. She then tells me to get her voice lessons when she's older because there's a definite talent there. Of course, I humbly agree.

The next step is to find out where *Star Search's* Ed McMahon grocery shops.

DAY 133

Sixteen pounds?!!!!

Actually, last night I weighed in at seventeen pounds above my prepregnancy starting point. But I'll go with the sixteen-pound figure today if given a choice between the two.

If given more of a selection to choose from, I'd choose not to have gained as much as I have. It's ironic. Family and friends tell me—unsolicited, naturally—that I don't look as if I've gained much. Of course, that is a relative statement. Gained much compared to what? But up until now, I've happily accepted their compliments without reading more into them.

Nevertheless, I'm not looking forward to my OB/GYN visit tomorrow morning because I think I've gained too much. Maybe I haven't. First, I'm going to ask to see my records from when I was pregnant with Courtney and see how I measure up. Second, I'll probably have to tell the doc I broke my nose four weeks ago. Then he'll probably give me that classic look. You know, the one that says, "I can't believe you're five months pregnant with a broken nose!"

It'll be easier than hearing him say, "I can't believe you're five months pregnant and have gained sixteen pounds!"

DAY 134

Nineteen pounds?!!!!

Well, *my* scales read sixteen pounds. Humph. But on the official records at Lewis-Gale Clinic, nineteen is the magic number after twenty-three weeks of pregnancy. I must add that they weighed me with shoes on.

Trying to salvage a bit of good news out of all this poundage, I asked the doctor today what I weighed at this time when I was pregnant with Courtney. I didn't salvage anything but more bad news. At twenty-six weeks I had gained a total of fourteen pounds. So if I don't gain an ounce in the next three weeks, I will be heavier by five pounds.

The doctor doesn't really seemed concerned. That's good news, I guess. He did tell me to be careful, as Thanksgiving and Christmas turkey dinners—and all that holiday munching in between—are just around the corner.

That has *me* concerned.

DAY 135

Well, we certainly discouraged one couple from having kids anytime soon.

We were entertaining a couple of newlyweds last night, and the evening was going smoothly until Courtney threw up.

DAY 136

Today I went for a part-time job interview, and I've got mixed emotions about it.

It was one of those things where I saw an interesting job in the paper, applied for it, and didn't expect anything to come from it.

Until they called me in for an interview.

I don't know if I got it. I don't know what I'd say if they offered it to me. I don't even know if I want it.

I guess I'm confused.

And I guess that's normal, since I've been out of the job market for more than a year. Notice I didn't say I've haven't *worked* in more than a year. I've worked harder without pay for more than a year than I did when I was pulling a paycheck.

Anyway, I guess I was just curious about this writing position, and the pay looked good—as far as writing positions go, not real jobs. But I really failed to look ahead to the possibility that they might actually want me, and I would have to choose between "full-time" motherhood and "part-time" motherhood, so to speak. If the latter, then I'd have to find suitable daycare. That really bothers me and makes me feel a little bit guilty.

What I do know is that I need an outside interest that takes my mind off whether or not Courtney had a dirty diaper today.

DAY 137

Okay, who's the wise guy?

I received a Frederick's of Hollywood catalog in the mail yesterday, full of stuff I'd be embarrassed to wear in the shower. And that's just the stuff I could identify. There were lots of things I'd have no idea how to wear—even if I did have a waist. Not to offend any of the fine folks at Frederick's, but some of the stuff didn't look like it was made too well. I mean, the material was awfully thin, see-through actually. And there were holes in places where I think there needed to be fabric.

Frankly, I'm at a stage in my life where I need more fabric than holes.

DAY 138

Today I write without a chair.

But I don't dare grumble about the inconvenience because right now Bryan's using my chair so he can wallpaper the bathroom. He's never wallpapered before. He wants me to help. I'm not in the wallpapering mood today. So he says he'll do it by himself. Then he discovers he needs me to help him hang the first strand or whatever wallpaper enthusiasts call it. Then he gets cranky because it's not hanging on the wall straight and starts to curdle.

Then he gets crankier when I point out to him that the paper's hanging upside down.

So he takes it down and tries again. Then he gets perturbed with me because I didn't line the paper up with the dotted lines he drew on the wall. I thought I did. So now I get cranky. On top of it all, it's difficult for me in my expanded condition to be very mobile in that tiny bathroom with Bryan being cranky and all. So I help him in his quest to hang the one piece and quietly exit the bathroom to keep peace in the family. I guess I'm doing it for my daughter and my unborn child.

But I sure would like my chair back.

DAY 139

I temporarily have my chair back.

Bryan's at the office right now, so he should have wallpapering off his brain. Unless he's thinking about ways to decorate his cubicle. Anyway, I reclaimed my chair out of the downstairs bathroom, where all this wallpapering (two strands, to be exact) has occurred, and put it back in front of the personal computer, where all my diary-writing takes place.

The last two weeks have been extremely hectic. Must have something to do with the Halloween season and all. Anyway, this week promises to be calmer, with my major project outside of my daily routine being to create Courtney's bunny ears. And of course, there's the matter of figuring out how to get her tail to stick onto her costume. Well, it's not a costume exactly; it's a white sweat suit, and I plan to put a wad of cotton on the seat as a tail. Cottontail, get it? Then I'll make up her face to look like a bunny. Getting her to sit still for that will be the major *challenge* of the week, however.

DAY 140

The family is sick today. Well, at least Bryan and I are, and

Courtney probably will be soon. Maybe she'll get lucky and miss it.

Yes, we're struck by the *D* word: diarrhea. I hear it's a twenty-four-hour thing. Bryan's ahead of me with about fifteen hours left of the bug. I've got an estimated twenty hours left. (All of this is on eastern standard time.)

All this reminds me of how rare it was for me to be sick when I was pregnant with Courtney—except morning sickness, of course. And come to think of it, this is the first time I've been sick while carrying this baby.

Instead of complaining, which I really wasn't, I should be thankful I've gone six-and-a-half months without much illness.

DAY 141

I'm proud of myself today.

For one thing, I lost two pounds. I guess I really can't take credit for that, though—it's the *D* word, you know. But that gave me an incentive to go to the gym this morning and work out even though I'm still a little sick.

At the heart of my workouts is the thirty-minute brisk walk. Since I've been pregnant and walking briskly, I've discovered I'm not a very good brisk walker. I'm a natural stroller. However, I think I've been increasing my pace—due to the peer pressure by skinny brisk walkers who do the "Y" regularly. These are the women who weigh 108 pounds (with their shoes on, no less), pin their hair up in flip ponytails, sport the latest in Spandex, and wear smug smiles on their faces that tell the not-very-brisk-walker they can walk circles around you.

I simply can't keep up. My shoes alone weigh 108 pounds, and I haven't been able to find maternity Spandex clothes. (Maybe Frederick's carries them.) But it helps me to be around them, to *try* to keep up and thus improve my own brisk walking ability.

Nevertheless, I'm still proud of myself today.

DAY 142

This morning, I reached the goal of all goals: getting my

twenty-nine-month-old daughter to sit on the potty.

That's all she did. Sit.

But it's definitely the first step in helping her cope with PPS—Pre-Potty Syndrome—as she has long refused to sit on her customized potty without a diaper for, lo, these past nine months. Well, that's not totally true. She has sat on the potty in the buff for my friend, Judy, who has a daughter nine months older than Courtney—several times, in fact. And to rub more baby powder in my wounded ego, even Bryan has persuaded Courtney to do the same on other occasions.

However, let me merely bring up the subject to Courtney and she runs out of the room screaming. Mention Mommy and potty in the same sentence, and Courtney needs a sedative. So for a long time, I put pottying on the back burner, until last night when Bryan bribed Courtney with the ultimate bribe: Barney.

Not Barney Fife. Barney the Dinosaur who hangs around with his Backyard Gang. It's a PBS show that's no longer carried here locally, but the rest of the world gets it. But we have tapes. Tapes that Courtney would do anything for, even sit on the potty.

You know, I'd sit on the potty, too, if I was offered something that neat—relatively speaking, of course. Like a two-week trip to Hawaii. Or tickets to the U.S. Open tennis tournament. Or being able to give birth to this baby I'm carrying with no pain whatsoever.

Now that I've got Courtney on the potty, what do I offer her next?

DAY 143

My chair's gone again.

Last night's Round Two of Wallpapering the Downstairs Bathroom That's Really Too Small to Hold Both Bryan and a Pregnant Woman went more smoothly than Round One.

And, more importantly, we're still married.

At the rate we're hanging the stuff, we're making this our fall project. And I realize the importance of this project. We definitely don't need to bring another child into this world without having our downstairs bathroom properly wallpapered.

When I gave birth to Courtney, we didn't even have a downstairs bathroom. The point is, if you have a downstairs bathroom, it's only appropriate to have it wallpapered. We did, by the way, have our two upstairs bathrooms wallpapered while I was pregnant with Courtney. We didn't do it ourselves. We hired the executive director of our city's chamber of commerce to do it for us. We see wallpapering as a white-collar job. Incidentally, this guy's now running for commissioner of the revenue.

He's got our vote.

DAY 144

I've starting the "nesting" process early.

Nesting is merely the maternal hormones kicking in just before the baby is born and makes the mom-to-be do weird things, like mop the floor. Well, that's weird for me because mopping is something I don't do until I get warning calls from the City Health Department.

But I'm supposedly at least three months away from this big clean-up event. Maybe what I'm experiencing is preterm nesting. I'm anxious to fix up Courtney's room-to-be, which is actually the guest room until I put the Barney the Dinosaur comforter on the bed, which will tell guests they can sleep in the new guest room downstairs, which is actually Courtney's toy room, but they can sleep there anyhow when we put the old guest room bed in the toy room. Right now the box springs is in the garage. We plan to keep the garage as the garage.

After all, there's no need to complicate things.

DAY 145

Today I have post-Halloween depression. Kind of like post-partum depression, except I haven't just had a baby and still have all that weight.

Well, I have gained a pound after going nearly two weeks without gaining any and in fact losing two during my brief bout with the *D* word.

It was fun to "create" a costume for Courtney and experience her first trick-or-treating extravaganza. She had fun, too. Now it's all over till next year, when I'll be creating for two.

DAY 146

Today is a red-letter day.

After four days of patiently waiting for Courtney to perform on the potty (I really do need to get out more or find a new hobby), she did it.

And I missed it.

Well, sort of. She tells me she wants to go to the potty as soon as we come home from grocery shopping. I oblige. Thinking that this would be another twenty-minute session of potty-sitting with no results and thinking about the $83.83 worth of groceries perishing in my Subaru in the garage, I tell Courtney to sit there and read her books while I get the groceries. She obliges. A few minutes later as I'm putting semi-thawed fish sticks in the freezer, Courtney shouts—with glee—"Mommy, look!" Sure enough, she did it. A tear came to my eye, and we shared a cappuccino moment. After this climactic potty event, I have just one question.

Now what?

DAY 147

What a more appropriate time to vote for president of the United States than the day after your two-year-old uses the potty for the first time!

Well, it has been a dirty campaign.

Today's election will determine who will be president when my unborn is born. From that standpoint, I view this election as more important than any other so far.

Anyway, I allowed my firstborn to be a part of the voting process. Before this morning, she hasn't had a chance to help me vote for president although she has participated in local and statewide elections. I allowed her to pull the levers, too, an exercise she found to be fun. Actually, she had less trouble voting than some people I've seen at the polls who pop their heads between the curtains to ask poll workers how to vote or what that bright light above the booth means or why the curtain won't open.

I even allowed Courtney to wear my "I Voted. Have You?" sticker. She's collecting stickers now and posting them on a piece of paper hanging on her door to indicate the number of times she's sat on the potty. Her voting sticker, by the way, is affixed next to the one that says "I'm a Big Sister."

DAY 148

My baby's going to be a Clinton baby, I guess.

But here's something that's even weirder. A woman *in labor* and on her way to the hospital stopped by the polls to vote.

I'm not so sure there shouldn't be a law for something like that. First of all, she should have voted absentee if her due date was going to fall on or near Election Day, especially since she obviously took voting so seriously as to risk giving birth in a voting booth. Second, don't you have to be sane or something to be eligible to vote? A woman in hard labor isn't exactly my picture of someone in a sane frame of mind.

I certainly wasn't sane during the labor stage with Courtney. I'm not too sure if I've even recovered my sanity, but that's another story. Anyway, on the way to the hospital about twenty-three minutes after my water broke, we decided to take a cake I baked the night before to the church building because we were scheduled to have a fellowship after services that morning. Like the fellowship of two hundred people couldn't go on as planned unless my cake was present. Okay, maybe I have this ego thing when it concerns my cakes. The church was not even on the way to the hospital, but about as opposite in direction as you could get. None of this classifies as sane thinking.

Makes me wonder if that woman voted for Clinton.

DAY 149

I've had a busy day of toilet training.

And when you're eight days away from entering your third trimester, you really are spending the day in the bathroom.

Actually, we are a week into pottying with Courtney. A week ago today, she sat on the potty in the buff for the first time. And today marks the fourth day in a row she's performed on the potty. And what's her reward? The satisfaction of accomplishment? The pleasant sensation of a dry diaper? Complete happiness knowing she's pleased Mom and Dad?

Nope. Thirty minutes of Barney the Dinosaur.

This past week I've been analyzing this toddler's transition from diaper to potty. Based on preliminary, nonscientific studies, this involves a startling political conclusion.

Courtney is Pro-Choice.

Courtney has—and will always strive to have—total control over her body, whether to use the potty or not.

As her mother, I have control over whether Courtney enters the bathroom door and on good days, whether she'll sit on the potty. Beyond that, it's like leading a horse to water, but you can't make him drink. In this scenario, you can lead the toddler to the potty, but you can't make her (insert bathroom language for potty function here).

I don't know whether it's politically correct to be Pro-Choice in potty matters; for now it's a fact I'll have to accept.

DAY 150

Sometimes I think it would be nice to have a soap opera baby.

First of all, you're pregnant for about five months—the length of time may be shorter depending on whether the actress is really pregnant and the writers have to work it into the script. During the gestation period, you look just as great as you did unpregnant—thanks to the talented artists in the makeup and costume departments.

Then, when it's time to have the baby, the labor lasts only an hour—beginning on the Friday episode and maybe stretching into Monday for ratings' sake. Yeah, there's pain, but I have yet to see a C-section.

Nobody takes these kids to a daycare center. Everybody on the soaps—even though they have outside-of-the-home jobs but don't ever seem to work—have home child care, only we don't know who actually cares for these children. And they surely don't stay young very long. Think of it in dog years. For each season, the kid ages seven years. In three years, they're twenty-one and have their own law practice. During that time, they grow on fast-forward and we see them only on holidays—July 4th, Thanksgiving, Christmas, and Veterans' Day. So we miss the teething, incessant spit-ups, potty training, temper tantrums, acne, etc.

But we also miss the first smile, first words, first steps, home-made gifts on Mother's and Father's Days, Little League, first date, high school graduation, etc.

Nah. Real-life babies are better, except maybe during the potty training stage.

Sixth Month

DAY 151

Sleeping is getting to be a drag.

For one thing, I drag my husband across the bed as I hold on to him to turn over. He says he sleeps through it. I guess I don't have much of an effect on him nowadays.

It seems I wake up about five or six times each night. I've memorized all the individual patterns in the wallpaper in the master bathroom and discovered minor blotches where pieces of wallpaper don't match up just exactly. It wouldn't be noticeable to the nonpregnant person making routine trips to the bathroom, only to those pregnant sorts who spend many of their waking—and nonwaking—hours there.

Incidentally, the guy who wallpapered our two upstairs bathrooms who ran for our city's commissioner of the revenue didn't win, but did receive eleven percent of the vote. I guess that means he wallpapered eleven percent of the bathrooms in town.

I wonder how many of that eleven percent were pregnant women who scrutinized his wallpapering-in-the-bathroom job?

DAY 152

Today is *my* day.

I'm going to Waynesboro, Virginia, to an outlet center to do a big hunk of my Christmas shopping. And I'm going *alone*.

Will I be lonely? Nope. Will I long for conversation? Nope. Will I keep hoping somebody will come up to me—maybe as I browse the Liz Claiborne racks—and ask me for apple juice? Nope. Will I worry whether a certain somebody has a dirty diaper or whether I should talk that same certain somebody into sitting on the potty? Nope. Will I try to hurry through the shops because another certain somebody—who may not have a dirty diaper or need persuasion to sit on the potty—wants to catch the Cowboys' game on TV? Nope.

That's because today is *my* day.

DAY 153

It's not my day anymore.

Mainly because it's Monday, a day *nobody* claims. It's a day set aside to pick up after the weekend. A day meant for doing the laundry, washing the dishes, mopping the floor, vacuuming the carpet, doing the grocery shopping, buying odds and ends at Wal-Mart, and working out. That's just what's planned before lunch.

And of course, it's just as hectic in the *paying* workplace. So hectic, in fact, there's the old saying that you shouldn't buy a car that was built on a Monday. I don't know how a consumer finds out something like that, though.

The same is probably true with babies. I don't have any scientific facts to back this one up, though it stands to reason. First of all, don't conceive on a Monday. That's easy enough.

When you think of how much you have to do on a Monday, there's neither time nor energy left for conceiving. Then, you shouldn't give birth on a Monday either. Doctors probably get Mondayitis, too, so hold off a day or manage to start labor early in the weekend to ensure a non-Monday delivery.

DAY 154

Well, I'm just days away from entering my third—and final—trimester. (Sound of trumpets herald this welcomed era of my pregnancy.)

And I'm beginning to feel the effects of this heavy stage, too. To begin with, it's a *heavy* stage. Just turning over in bed registers a 6.7 on the Richter scale. Breathing, as I've mentioned earlier I think, is sometimes a chore, but only during particular times, like when I'm trying to sleep. Plus, I'm really showing now. Let's see, what word comes to mind when I look in the mirror?

Barn.

But I'm thankful to be on the edge of the third trimester because this is how I'm *supposed* to feel during the last three months.

DAY 155

I'm eating a "Fun Size" Milky Way at this very moment.

Actually, I'd be having more fun if I were eating a regular size Milky Way.

But when you're as pregnant as I am, fun means "...a tiny piece of chocolate that's just a fraction of the size of a real Milky Way, and you get to enjoy it for about twenty-two seconds (or two bites, whichever comes first), but you'll still have to ride the exercise bike at the gym for forty-six minutes to burn off the fatty calories you just wolfed down, and if you're pregnant, forget it, because you're going to get bigger anyway whether you ride the bike or not."

Okay, so maybe I'm a little down today about working out. I'm used to *seeing* results of my exercise efforts. All I see nowadays is the climbing needle on my bathroom scales (which, to make matters worse, are four pounds below the doctor's).

Bryan keeps encouraging me, however. *His* needle isn't climbing, so it's easy for him to do so. But deep down beneath all this baby fat, I appreciate him for encouraging me anyway.

DAY 156

I'm at the point now in my pregnancy where I don't do tubs.

Then again, I've been at the point of not doing tubs for the past six years. There is nothing attractive about cleaning a bathtub. Do you ever see Cindy Crawford hunched over a scum-ridden tub with a can of Comet in one hand and a scouring pad in the other? I think not.

In fact, when it comes to any kind of cleaning (the kind that has to be done before the Board of Health comes knocking at my door), I prefer no one see me doing it. Especially Bryan. I'd rather him think that the house never gets dirty than to think I clean it.

Maybe that's a weird point of view, but I didn't attract my man to begin with by showing him my vacuuming techniques.

DAY 157

Today is the beginning of my last trimester, the day I enter my seventh month of pregnancy, the day I shout "Hurrah!" as I start the home stretch.

Stretch *marks* is more like it.

Of course, I never fully got rid of the stretch marks from birthing Courtney. And now I'll get a fresh batch of stretch marks to go with the ones I still have. I hope they're at least color-coordinated.

DAY 158

Department stores depress me.

All the mannequins have waists—skinny waists I never had *before* my childbearing years and I will never have *because* of my childbearing years. Even the maternity mannequins have a more defined waist than I do. But these maternity mannequins are in no way anatomically correct. The most obvious anatomical error in these simulated plastic pregnant bodies is the lack of sufficient fatty layers *all over*.

Let's get real. These aren't *real* women. Real women not only don't eat quiche, but they also have real pregnancies. And those twenty-five to thirty pounds you're supposed to gain during those nine months are not deposited in one place. Otherwise, we'd be talking about one BIG baby! Or at least, two small babies.

Naturally, all this negates a maternity mannequin that retains water, which means you won't see one with swollen ankles and blown-up knees. Big busts are out, too.

So I'm trying to avoid the malls during this last trimester because all this fiction is really getting to me.

DAY 159

This baby is very active, and if I didn't know better (which I admit I don't always), I'd think I'm further along than I am. Of course, I might be, but I won't know until I have him/her.

I've found that this baby wakes up every time I eat a Reese's Peanut Butter Cup, one of the food groups I've been indulging in a lot lately.

When the baby moves, it makes me even more aware of the miracle that's growing inside me. Bryan enjoys being a part of it, too, always wanting to feel the baby kick or elbow me in the ribs. I let Courtney feel the baby, although I'm not sure she knows what she's feeling. But to include her in this experience is important and to make her aware of her soon-to-be new role of big sister is probably more important.

DAY 160

The major question of the day: do I wear my pink sweat pants or my black ones?

I've delegated each pair an assignment. I own three pairs of pink sweats, all of which accommodate my expanded girth. One pair is for sleeping, another is for daily wear and tear around the house (in case I get the uncontrollable urge to vacuum or something), and the other is for working out. My black ones are multi-purpose, capable of being worn for any of the above activities. The black pair, incidentally, was part of my wardrobe I wore to the hospital just moments after my water broke when I had Courtney. They've been laundered since then.

Speaking of laundry, that's a task I've had to perform more frequently in these last few months due to a lack of clothes. But I'm not complaining.

Well, if I *had* to complain, I'd gripe about how I can barely fit between the dryer door when I open it and the wall. Hopefully, this will pass in three months.

But what will I complain about then?

DAY 161

I've concluded that pregnant women are wiser the second time around.

Not that I've put much of my wisdom to use, but I'm talking specifically about the stuff moms and dads buy for the baby—and the baby hasn't the foggiest idea what they've bought him.

Nevertheless, parents and other well-meaning relatives and friends get sucked into the *baby racket*. Subliminally, they're made to feel guilty if they don't buy all the baby stuff ever marketed—from a bear that makes womb sounds ($50) to a stroller made for active moms to push around when they jog ($350). I remember a fleet-footed dad pushing his tot strapped in one of those three-wheeled contraptions who beat me by several minutes in a 5K race. That isn't saying too much though: the guy who won the 10K that same day was just seconds behind me—and we started at the same time!

DAY 162

I'm not finished discussing the unnecessary stuff we buy for newborns. Of course I probably would've been had I not gone off on a tangent about the guy with the jogging stroller who beat me in that 5K race.

Let's talk clothes. It's important to note that not many

newborns wear size 0-3 months, and if they do they won't wear them for three months. I recommend starting them off with comfortable, non-binding outfits sized 3-6 or even 6-9 months.

How many clothes to buy? That depends on how many clothes are given to you. But keep in mind infants who lay around in a bed, playpen, activity blanket, or your arms all day don't wear out their clothes. You won't find holes in their socks after a few months. But they might get dirty—soiled is the proper baby term. So how many clothes you have on hand depends also on how many times you want to do laundry.

DAY 163

Traveling is now more difficult in this last trimester.

Bathrooms are a precious commodity. Clean ones are worth even more.

Forget about napping in the car. I've discovered my body no longer bends in certain places like it used to in order to get into a comfortable sleep position.

Sitting upright in the car agitates the baby, who tries to squirm and kick me so I'll give him/her more interior space. Maybe Bryan should just strap my belly on top of the car and hang a WIDE LOAD sign to the bumper.

DAY 164

It's so much fun taking a two-and-a-half-year-old to my monthly OB/GYN visit…by myself. Especially on the same day I have to have lab work done.

Take the glucola test, for example. That's where you drink a super-sugary drink, and then an hour later they draw your blood for tests. Courtney wanted some of my "juice." The last four months of sharing lessons go down the drain as I tell her she can't have my "juice" and unsuccessfully tell her why not. Like she really understands these things.

Then you have to wait the hour, but that's the easy part because everybody in the waiting room thinks your child is cute and inadvertently helps to entertain her. Then it's time to go and wait some more in a less favorable atmosphere, the examining room. It's during this time Courtney explores the instruments, medicines, and the latest in technology used by OB/GYNs. She particularly likes the blood pressure machine and the K-Y Jelly. Naturally, as I'm sitting on the table half-naked, and thus half-powerless over her youthful curiosity, she occasionally runs into the stirrups and bumps her head.

That's probably when females really begin to hate those things.

DAY 165

It's happened already: I've got the "pregnant waddle."

Kind of like the bunny hop, except no one better dare stick a cotton ball on my backside.

I first noticed it during a recent trip to Kmart; I needed to buy some strapping tape. Walking, or rather waddling, across the parking lot and toward the glass doors, I saw my penguin-like reflection and immediately thought, "Hey, what's that pregnant lady who can't walk upright without waddling from side to side doing in my reflection?" My next thought was to complain to the manager.

Then I became aware of how motorists stop when I approach a crossing, and oftentimes I'm not close enough to the crossing to warrant their stopping to let me cross. Then I become self-conscious because I can't cross as fast as I used to cross and all these people are watching me cross.

And on top of that, I really don't cross. I waddle.

DAY 166

I've started reading again.

This time I decided to delve into the past—the way-long-ago past—and learn about pregnancy and childbirth throughout history. Those were times when pregnant women didn't take horse pills to keep up with their vitamin needs and didn't know the meaning of the word "epidural."

And from everything I've learned so far, I really appreciate that I do know the meaning of that word.

Lots of pain, often accentuated by "well-meaning" mid-wives and doctors who frankly didn't know what we know today about birthing a baby. Lots of grabbing and pulling and tugging, and for the sake of not scaring mothers-to-be, I won't say what they were grabbing, pulling and tugging. And lots of bloodletting during the pregnancy itself, something about keeping the mother's body "clean" from impurities and disease that could harm the baby.

Maternity leave?

Ha. Working women a few hundred years ago worked in the field often up to the time of their first labor pains, went somewhere to have it, rested maybe—just maybe—a couple of days, and back into the field they went. Don't bother asking if those couple of days were *paid* maternity leave.

I have trouble picturing these very pregnant women working for long periods of time in the fields to begin with.

Pregnant Port-O-Johns maybe?

DAY 167

Remember that scene in *Gone with the Wind* where Scarlett and all the other women were told to go upstairs right in the middle of that swell party and take a nap?

That's how I felt today. Except there wasn't any party with men in gray suits and ascot ties sitting around talking about the possibility of war and women in size three petticoats trying to get their attention. And certainly none of those females were pregnant. (Frankly, my dear, I don't think film producers in the '30s were allowed to show pregnant women.)

Anyway, Bryan told me to take a nap. I wasn't sleepy. He insisted. Instead of a war going on, I think he simply wanted to see some football game on TV. With me safely tucked into bed, he could watch without me griping about watching the game, which is something I don't do, but I guess he has this phobia that I will, though.

I think it's called Nagaphobia.

DAY 168

Honestly, I think I could eat a whole side of beef in one sitting nowadays.

All of a sudden, my appetite has really increased to bounds I'm not sure I'm capable of handling without entering the world of gluttony. I could eat incessantly all day if given the chance, and unfortunately, if it weren't for sleep, I would have all day to do so. But now I have about 15 hours to eat nonstop.

I told Bryan to put a muzzle on me. Not literally, of course. He probably couldn't find a maternity muzzle for me anyway. But he did say he'd help me curb my eating binges, constantly reminding me of how hard I'm going to have to work out at the gym to work off the extra pregnancy weight after the baby is born.

But that's *months* away. When my body calls for two bowls of Cap'n Crunch Berries at 10 P.M., I'm going to answer it.

DAY 169

A lot of people at church the other day seemed to be relieved that I finally look pregnant.

Finally? My mirror tells me I've looked pregnant since my third *week*. But I guess it would be rather self-centered of me to think friends, family, and mere acquaintances have been charting the progress of my body since I announced my pregnant condition. Like they actually have a chart taped to their refrigerator entitled, "Karen's Weight and Measurements During Her Pregnancy," which hangs next to a picture of Noah and the ark that their kids colored in Sunday School.

Maybe not. However, I must've looked awfully pregnant that day, and I attribute that look to my awfully pregnant-looking dress that hung on my body like a tent. It's one of those jumpers made of faded denim with a sash in the back. There's really no purpose in the sash, except to make me look like I'm in the third grade. So maybe compared to the other maternity clothes—and nonpregnant, oversized clothes—I'd been wearing up until then, I did look bigger than before.

So what about that dress? It may be the only thing I can squeeze into by my ninth month, so I'll hang on to it. After that, I'm going to donate it to the Girl Scouts of America; maybe they can use it for overnight camping trips.

DAY 170

Today is Thanksgiving, my favorite holiday of the year.

One thing I like to do on this day is to make a list—even write it down—of things I'm thankful for. This year is no exception:

• My husband and daughter
• And another one on the way
• Family and friends
• Warm house, plenty of food, clothes, all the basic necessities of life
• The luxuries of life, too—cars, vacations, etc.
• My health and the fact I haven't gained 30 pounds yet

I stop to wonder what my life will be like next Thanksgiving—another one at the table to pass the food. He or she will be nine months by then and perhaps will be *throwing* food across the table.

DAY 171

The name-game continues.

This time, I checked out a more up-to-date baby name book from the library, one that didn't claim that Ashley is a boy's name. Separately and together, Bryan and I thumbed through it. (We didn't bother to consider names beginning with some letters, like *I*, *E*, and sometimes *Y*.)

It didn't help.

But I think Bryan will give in to my boy's name suggestion of Kyle. He had been stubbornly insistent that we name him Tyler, a name far too popular nowadays to suit me. However, he likes Monica for a girl's name. I liked it before we came up with Courtney's name, but I've been indifferent to it this time around. I'm afraid we're at a stalemate here, so it's back to the negotiating table. Perhaps he'll suddenly remember somebody in his childhood he really detested named Kyle and nix it if I don't go along with Monica.

Hope is on the horizon. The other day, I asked him about Adrienne, a name I like and have brought up a couple of times. He said he likes it, but he's still clinging to Monica.

What this tells me is that I'm carrying a boy—because we

are a lot closer to solving the boy's name dilemma than we are the girl's. Thus, we'll sweat and toil over it for the next two-and-a-half months, pout, and even argue some, until either one of us concedes defeat or we come to some sort of compromise. We'll go through all of the above only to find out we didn't have to.

I think that comes under Murphy's Law of Naming Babies.

DAY 172

Today Bryan and I are celebrating our anniversary.

Except it's not our anniversary.

Rather, it's the only convenient time we can leave Courtney at Grandma's, find a cozy bed and breakfast inn in the Blue Ridge Mountains, and not interfere too much with my pregnant schedule. That is, I don't want to be deep in the mountains away from civilization (my hospital and doctor and all that deductible insurance money we've spent so far) as I get really close to my due date. And our anniversary right after Christmas will put me within six weeks of my due date.

I say let's stay home for the holidays this year.

DAY 173

The books tell me that the baby at this point of my pregnancy weighs about three pounds.

Makes me wonder about that extra twenty or so pounds that's clinging to me now. Makes me wonder how much more nonbaby weight I'm going to gain in two-and-a-half months. Makes me wonder what I'm going to do with that extra weight. And if I decide to lose it, makes me wonder *how*?

But at this point in my pregnancy, wondering is about all I do. I've long since left the fretting stage, way back when all I gained was four pounds and I was still wearing normal clothes.

Now my clothes are anything but normal. Ever notice the strange prints on maternity clothes? Looks like rejected material from the American Tablecloth Factory. I think that's located somewhere up north, like in Pennsylvania. Nobody has to look at my pear-shaped figure to figure out that I'm pregnant.

Nope. Just look at the tacky prints on my shirts, something I definitely wouldn't wear on my normally size-nine body.

But at this point in my pregnancy, it brings me back to wondering. Makes me wonder how much longer I'll not really care about what I'm wearing.

DAY 174

I don't think Bryan and I are the bed-and-breakfast type.

But I don't care. Remember, at six-and-a-half months along, there aren't too many things I care about anymore—except having a healthy baby...and having it *soon*.

Anyway, every time we go to a B&B inn, Bryan tells me the people who stay there are "snooty." That's kind of a prejudiced, unfair, and rude thing to say. He likes staying at the inn, but not mingling with the other guests.

Until this weekend, Bryan's been lucky—he hasn't had to eat breakfast at the same table with other people (except me, but he knew that would happen when he married me).

But then it happened—he had to eat with other people. Gasp. And it wasn't like we were sitting down to bowls of corn flakes, either. Nope, we're talking about a meal that began with a sour grapefruit and five eating utensils. (I don't use utensils to eat my Pop Tarts at home.)

It got better, however. The blueberry pancakes were the best I'd ever eaten. The bacon was tasty, too. (Of course, it's hard to mess up bacon.) It's just that I felt funny cutting the bacon with a knife and fork because that's what everyone else, save Bryan, was doing. In essence, I succumbed to the peer pressure.

We survived the meal, but we had to deal with the conversation, which bounced from adobe villages in Santa Fe to some fancy classical music festival in Charleston, South Carolina. I can converse with the best of them, although how I responded did not necessarily reflect my thoughts.

Example 1: The wives were bragging about their husbands' kitchen talents, how they do the cooking, and how they are fabulous at mixing the right spices and creating culinary wonders.

My response: A simple nod as if I could relate to that.

What I was *really* thinking: Bryan can make spaghetti, mixing just the right amount of Ragu sauce, hamburger meat and noodles.

Example 2: The couples were comparing notes on how they each decorated their children's rooms. One did an authentic western motif, complete with artifacts from the Old West.

My response: A simple nod as if I could relate to that.

What I was *really* thinking: We did Courtney's room in modern-day *Barney*.

They were nice people, albeit a little weird, and we appreciated the opportunity to get acquainted with them over grapefruit.

DAY 175

The time has come to slow down the workouts.

I became overly exhausted after my usual workout on the steps and bike—actually, a little under what I normally do. I was too tired to briskly walk for thirty minutes.

That concerns me—to think I was too worn out to walk briskly. So I'm eliminating the steps and bike and sticking with the brisk walk.

I can't give up now. I may not care as much about my weight gain (today, I'm twenty-five pounds above prepregnancy weight) as much as I was months ago, but I set a goal: to work out 'til labor sets in.

DAY 176

Here's another one to file under Old Pregnant Wives' Tales: Pregnant women have a keener immune system and don't get sick.

Ha.

I'm sick, although I'm not sure with what. I don't think it's the flu, but it's at least a nasty cold. Then again, most colds are probably nasty. Ever heard of a lovely cold?

Courtney's sick, too. Hers has an official diagnosis: croup. That can be more scary for the parent than the child. Luckily, her case isn't dangerous. She just feels rotten, like I do. So we've spent the day wallowing in our illnesses and watching *Sesame Street* and *Barney* videos. You know you're really sick when you discover the *Eight is Enough* Christmas episode (that's the one where thieves steal the Bradfords' station wagon), and you don't bother to change channels!

You also don't bother to take a shower. I may be sleeping on the sofa tonight—Bryan's sense of smell is a lot keener than my immune system.

DAY 177

When you're nearly seven months pregnant, there's nothing like good socks.

I've discovered good socks when you're pregnant are a lot different from when you're not pregnant. Good socks have to be easy to put on. That means you don't have to be able to touch your feet in order to put them on. I haven't touched my feet in two months.

So it's wise to avoid the anklets.

DAY 178

I hope Courtney changes her sleeping habits before she gets married.

This week during her bout with croup, I've slept with her because that's the thing moms do. Perhaps "slept" isn't the best way to put it—maybe "attempted to sleep."

And it hasn't been a comfortable attempt.

Why? To begin with, it's difficult enough to sleep when you're nearly seven months pregnant anyway. It becomes more difficult when you have to sleep with 104 stuffed animals and a two-and-a-half-year-old child in a double bed, when you're spoiled by usually sleeping with a twenty-nine-year-old guy and no stuffed animals in your own queen-size bed. I don't care if there are purple-and-green pictures of Barney the Dinosaur all over the comforter. It's not that much of a comfort to me. Then, that same two-and-a-half-year-old refuses to sleep length-wise on her side of the bed. She prefers to sleep perpendicular, with her head rammed into my ribs and feet hanging over the bedrail. Further, the other side of my pregnant body is squashed against the bedrail. The situation gets uglier when I have to get up to go to the bathroom thirteen times during the night.

I don't know if Courtney appreciates all of this sacrifice. I'm sure she doesn't recognize the bags under my eyes from lack of sleep on her behalf. But if she becomes a mother herself one day, it'll come back to her, and then she will.

DAY 179

I'm beginning to realize that Courtney needs a brother or sister.

She's bored with us.

Not exactly bored, but it's time she got to know other members of our family, specifically the one I'm carrying. However, I'm concerned over her reaction once the newborn arrives. She's made it plain to me she doesn't like me to hold my friends' babies.

So I've been doing some more reading, this time about new babies and older siblings. These articles encourage sibling participation in the rearing of the new baby. For example, let the child help mom with changing the baby's diapers. Courtney doesn't even want me to change *her* diapers, so I doubt she'll be a willing participant in this activity.

Perhaps she will want to help sing the baby to sleep. Of course, this could develop into a bad habit, meaning the baby will end up not sleeping unless Courtney sings to her. Courtney's at that two-and-a-half-year-old temperamental stage when I can't count on her to perform every time I want her to.

I think I'll give Courtney opportunities to help out but not push her into any heavy responsibility. I don't think I could handle it.

DAY 180

It's newsletter time again.

It's time to realize my pregnancy is moving right along and to realize time is running out to get everything done I want to before Number Two arrives.

This newsletter—focusing on the eighth month, which begins next week—is somewhat comforting. Sort of. It says, "Layers of insulating fat are building up under the skin…" It doesn't say *whose* skin, so I'll have to assume it's mine. I do feel somewhat warmer than those around me in this thirty-degree weather we've had recently. So far it's not enough to make me rush out and buy a maternity coat. Of course it helps, too, that a friend lent me a winter cape that I'll wear if we enter another ice age before this one arrives.

The newsletter further points out that this is the month couples start to realize they're going to be parents. We're already parents, but Bill Cosby comes to mind when I think about the arrival of this baby: he says (something to this effect) there's a big difference in having a child versus having *children*.

In preparation for our multiple children, we've been taking care of our friends' two daughters, who have about the same age difference as Courtney and the baby will have. We have learned a lot. In fact, that's what we're doing right now. Well, I was doing it, but now Bryan's doing it, so I can write in my diary to tell about what it's like.

Seventh Month

DAY 181

I'm not looking forward to my doctor's visit tomorrow.

It's the scales thing, you know.

I lucked out during my last visit three weeks ago. They were in the middle of moving their offices so they weighed me on those old-fashioned balance scales instead of the high-tech digital ones. I've never given any credence to the latter. In essence, I didn't gain as much as those digital scales would've said I did.

They probably have the digital scales plugged in by now, and there's no avoiding that, I suppose. So my weight gain for the last three weeks is going to appear more than what I really gained.

I sense a lecture from my doctor about the hazards of late-night bowls of Sugar Smacks and Cap'n Crunch Berries.

DAY 182

No lecture. In fact, I really didn't gain that much at all since my last visit to the doc.

It was a rather uneventful session with my OB/GYN. I kind of like it that way. He said the baby and I are right on schedule growth-wise and the heartbeat sounded strong. His only concern was my *other* end: my head. I've had a cold or something for more than a week, and it has moved into my larynx, which means I've got laryngitis.

The doc promptly gave me a prescription for amoxycillin— not the bubble-gum flavored stuff Courtney gets; I have to take the pill form, which isn't as tasty and is more likely to gag me. But I do appreciate the doc's concern.

I just wish he'd prescribed medicine that tasted good, too.

DAY 183

I don't believe it. People who've heard through the grape-vine that I'm pregnant are coming up to me and asking me if I'm pregnant.

Of course, that's a personal question, but I answer it anyway. I ran into an acquaintance whom I don't see but twice a year at Wal-Mart or Kroger, and she told me she'd heard I was pregnant.

I said, "Very."

Perplexed, she looked me up and down. I made it easier on her and flashed open my windbreaker, which doesn't close all the way anymore, and gave her a side profile glimpse of my seven months of pregnancy.

At seven months, I shouldn't have to go around proving my condition. I'm beyond that and deserve the recognition of being a woman with child, thus receiving all sorts of respect— from both friends and strangers. I've gained twenty-six pounds that I'm going to pay dearly for in a few months, so give me the proper respect all pregnant women deserve.

DAY 184

I'm finally getting over this nasty cold, and Courtney's much better, too.

I defied my doc's suggestion about getting the amoxycillin and decided to let this one take its course. If he'd prescribed it to me ten days ago, then maybe I'd have taken him up on his suggestion. Hopefully, this will be the only time I'll get sick this season, at least before the baby is born.

DAY 185

A friend once told me—after Courtney was born but way before I got pregnant again—to decide whether to have another child before Courtney turned eighteen months old, because then I wouldn't want any more kids as she approached the Terrible Twos. (Courtney, that is, not my friend.) At eighteen months, it turned out, Courtney was real cute. She was real cute again at two years, causing me to naïvely think she was going to by-pass that feared stage.

Yeah, right.

Well, she's there now, and there's no turning back. At two-and-a-half, she's at the point where you can dress her up but you can't take her anywhere. Like Kmart. It's not like Kmart is one of those quiet places where everyone is watching you and you can't touch anything. You don't even have to dress up for Kmart. Nope. The only responsibility Courtney has is to sit in a buggy.

Courtney, a child who normally likes a good buggy ride, didn't like it one bit today. Her tantrum could be heard for miles.

So I guess you could say today Courtney had a bad-buggy day.

DAY 186

Today is the last day of my seventh month. Only fifty-seven shopping days until the birth of my second born.

Which reminds me. I need to order birth announcements. We're into the cutesy announcements, cards that reflect something about our personalities, jobs, hobbies, etc. To announce Courtney's entrance into this world, we got cards that said, "Announcing a New Tennis Star."

I think this time we're going with a golf theme. But I haven't ordered the cards yet. I can't forget to do so.

We also can't forget to decide on a name. Baby Nutt just won't cut it. At present, we're mulling over Kyle and Monica. Kyle's fine with me, but I'm not so sure about Monica, and Bryan is just the opposite with these names.

It might just be a last-minute decision, however. I remember deciding on Courtney's middle name on the operating table, but at least we had the first name decided. We know the boy's middle name; he'll take Bryan's middle name, McMillan. Needless to say, we have no idea on the girl's middle name because we can't decide on the first name and middle names are dependent on first names.

I think we're in a dilemma.

DAY 187

The countdown has started.

With Courtney we started the countdown at the beginning of the eighth month, and we'll carry on this Nutt tradition with this one, as well.

And like Courtney's due date, I'm sure this baby's due date will be here in no time. Courtney was also eight days late. I have a feeling this one will be at least eight days early. I don't know how much of that is my own intuition and how much is what people have been telling me. Stuff like, "You always have the second one earlier." That comment ranks up there with, "You always gain more with the second one than with the first."

And that's not comforting. But having this one before the due date wouldn't be so bad because being pregnant is not one of my favorite things to do, and by the ninth month, if I recall, it was at the bottom of my Favorite Things To Do list.

DAY 188

It's happened.

I've turned into my mother.

The other day Courtney wanted to do something. I don't remember what. That's not important now. What's important is my response to her request, which for a two-and-a-half-year-old is probably more like a *demand.*

"We'll see," I told her.

As those words flowed from my mouth, memories of my own "We'll see" pasts came flowing to my mind. I remembered how much I couldn't stand for my mother to tell me "We'll see." Actually, my father said that a lot, too, so I've really turned into my *parents*, not just my mother.

That's scary.

Now I'm passing on the "We'll see" tradition to my own child. Like an old fruitcake recipe.

DAY 189

I've been thinking lately about how fortunate I am to live in these high-tech times.

Pregnancy speaking, that is.

Of course, there's nothing high-tech about being pregnant; that's been going on since the Monroe Administration. (Remember the Era of Good Feeling?) But many mysteries of pregnancy are revealed through high-tech procedures.

Such as the due date. Long before the advent of birth control pills, which typically regulate periods to precise days, women would not only get pregnant more times than they would like, but they also wouldn't know *when* they would have the baby.

Horrors.

I take my due date as gospel, knowing full well the concept of a due date is to give the pregnant woman an idea of when the baby's due and knowing the baby will probably arrive anywhere from two weeks before that date to two weeks after. In other words, a twenty-eight-day spread.

But I'd still be lost without a date to talk about.

DAY 190

"Boy, it sure is nice to see a clean house," my husband said.

Problem is, he didn't say it to *me*.

He said it to a couple whom we were visiting at the time. I'm not too sure I would have appreciated that comment had he said it to me to begin with…makes it seem like my house is rarely clean. Which is true, but I don't need him to point it out to me. However, let me interject that the Health Department has never issued me a citation.

But it's worse to air our dirty house to people we don't know very well at all. These are people who've never seen my house so they could object to such a comment.

After Bryan said what he said, the look of embarrassment on my face apparently caused him to elaborate on his poorly phrased statement.

"What I mean is, you don't have toys lying around," he feebly added to get out of the hole he had dug.

Needless to say, this couple doesn't have kids. If this couple did, they certainly wouldn't be *normal* kids because toys are supposed to be lying around.

I don't know if they know that, though.

DAY 191

I believe the last trimester is God's way to get the mom-to-be used to another child.

I call it, for a lack of a better term, the "Tied Down Syndrome."

From the beginning of the seventh month and lasting through that final labor pain, an "anchor" develops around the tummy, hindering mom from being as active as she once was.

Drop anchor, and mom discovers she still can't be as active as she once was.

All this becomes more magnified when she's pregnant with her second child.

Take this morning, for example. I believe Courtney's purpose for our trip to the Baby Superstore was to test the strength of my anchor. Totally absorbed in the Barney doll collection the store displayed, Courtney refused to come along with me when it was time to depart. In fact, she fled in the opposite direction.

I fled after her, doing a very good impression of a penguin. As I was doing a fast waddle up and down aisles, Courtney continued to evade me, until I—with my bachelor's degree in journalism—outsmarted her and cut her off at the pass, or rather at the infant sleepwear section.

Then Courtney pulled Plan B—lie down on the floor and scream. This was tougher than the chase, especially when I have trouble picking up anything below my quickly disappearing bellybutton.

As I picked her up (realizing by this time there's a lady charging admission to this scene), she let her body go limp, making herself into a twenty-nine-pound rag doll. I had no other choice but to give her a strong dose of discipline and make a fast exit—no encores, please.

In retrospect, I know that this is a taste of what life will be with two children because when this other one's born, I'll slowly regain my speed and agility, but at the same time I'll have another anchor that'll slow me down.

I look forward to the challenge.

DAY 192

It's a week before Christmas, and all through the house, not a toddler was whining, not even Courtney.

That's all I want for Christmas this year.

I just keep reminding myself that Courtney's going through a phase, kind of like an extended version of PMS—Perennial Moodiness Syndrome.

But her two-and-a-half-year-oldness makes me appreciate the times she really is sweet and adorable, which is what she really is down deep underneath the tantrums and incessant whining fits.

For example, last year she refused to sit on Santa's lap. This year she refused to sit on Santa's lap. Last year she kicked, screamed, and caused a scene. This year she merely stood beside Santa, telling him from a faraway distance that all she wants for Christmas is a new stuffed lamb and a bottle of juice. (She's not getting the lamb; we can't find one like the one she has. Instead, she's getting a bowling set.)

The video of last year's Santa visit is not a pleasant sight due to the screaming (mine and Courtney's), but this year's tape is more palatable, as the brattiest she gets is when she pushes away the candy cane Santa tries to give her. She then tells him she's sleepy. Yet, I'm happy with the strides she made to reconcile herself to the Santa Man and I cherish these calmer, quieter moments in her life nowadays.

Next year, I suspect, will be an improvement even over this year, and that's something to look forward to.

And then, two years from now, I can look forward to more of the same from last year.

DAY 193

Hide 'n seek is a sport I'll have to discontinue until after this baby is born.

For three reasons: 1) I'm limited where I can hide. After a couple of rounds, folks can easily narrow down the places where I can feasibly put myself. 2) I'm limited where I can seek. And if I do seek someone, that nonpregnant someone is probably faster than I am right now and can easily beat me to the base. 3) I make too much noise when I hide and when I seek.

Why? Simply because my thighs have now grown together and create a thunderous swishing sound when I walk. So, obviously, corduroy pants are out of the question.

But my corduroys are one of the remaining three pairs of pants I can still squeeze into.

And I value my limited wardrobe much more than I do hide 'n seek.

DAY 194

My name is Karen, and I'm a cereal addict.

The only time I can control my addiction is during the lunch hour, when I usually chow down on a turkey and American cheese sandwich. So Cap'n Crunch Berries doesn't make a good side dish.

But it sure does late at night, and of course in the morning.

Part of it, I'm sure, has to do with the said pregnancy cravings. The other part is pure addiction. A habit I'm not willing to kick.

Generally, I will not eat the same cereal twice in one day, especially if I'm driving. For example, I may eat Sugar Smacks or Cap'n Crunch Berries for breakfast and Rice Krispies at night—the snap, crackle and pop keeps me awake long enough to eat it.

DAY 195

It's been a while, but I finally hit the track again.

And, boy, I could tell it's been a while!

But I'm proud of myself for going to my workout, although my workout doesn't seem to be much of a workout anymore. For one thing, I can't work out long enough to work up a sweat, which is probably good. It's only bad in my mind when I think about how much sweating I did months ago.

(Incidentally, pregnant women in their last trimester don't sweat: they glow.)

By merely showing up at the gym this morning, I've surpassed my exercise routine when I was pregnant with Courtney. If I recall—and that's all I can do since I didn't keep a diary then—I exercised vigorously until about the fifth month. After that, I hit a few tennis balls or shot a few hoops with Bryan. I do definitely without a doubt recall beating my athletic husband in a couple of games of "horse" forty-eight hours before Courtney was born. Knowing Bryan, I know he didn't let me win, either, for fear of making such public, like I'm doing right now.

However, my workout now consists of one element: the brisk walk. It's also not as brisk as it was five months ago, but it will do. I walk along a small track that's 1/26th of a mile long, which gives me a good idea how hamsters who go 'round and 'round on that little Ferris wheel feel.

I wonder how pregnant hamsters work out.

DAY 196

Maybe I'm just more sensitive because I'm pregnant during

this holiday season, but some things really are getting on my nerves lately.

Like the verse in the Christmas song that goes, "...I don't know if there'll be snow, but have a cup of cheer."

That really bugs me.

What does figuring out the weather have to do with having a cup of cheer? And what's cheer? Eggnog? Boiled custard? Punch-like stuff with ice cream in it? Or should it be capitalized, meaning that someone needs to do the laundry?

Then there's the Christmas song that lacks originality in its title, called "The Christmas Song." That's the one where only people falling within a certain age group receive Christmas greetings: "...and though I'm offering this simple phrase, for kids from one to ninety-two...Merry Christmas to you." Even if they were just going for a rhyme there, they could've been more inclusive and said kids up to 122. The oldest living person currently is 114 (which doesn't rhyme), but it allows more leeway.

"Up on the housetop reindeer pause. Out jumps good ol' Santa Claus..." Jumping out from where? Then like a lot of other Santa Claus songs, it goes on to talk about going up and down chimneys. (The Santa whom Courtney stood beside this year kept calling it a "chimley.")

We don't have a chimney. Or a chimley. Which means I'm already getting caught up in my tales of Santa Claus. Our Santa comes in the front door. He has his own key because otherwise we'd end up paying bundles to fix the lock.

Then I have to tell Courtney we don't have a chimney because we have central air.

DAY 197

I got a good report from my bi-weekly visit to the doctor yesterday.

Everything is progressing smoothly at thirty-two-and-a-half weeks, the doctor will let me travel to Tennessee over the holidays, and I've gained three pounds. At this rate, I'll probably hit or barely surpass the weight I gained with Courtney.

And the baby has turned upside down, getting ready to be born.

That's scary.

That means it won't be long until baby makes four. That means we're in the home stretch—or stretch marks. That means we'll soon have another mouth to feed. That means we'll have to fork out $124,538 to raise this baby. That means we'll be totally responsible for all aspects of this child's life. That means we'll have another baby to potty train.

That also means I'll soon be losing all this weight!

DAY 198

If I have my way, this is the last trip I'm taking while pregnant.

Right now, we're embarking on an eight-hour trip to Nashville, but I'm confident there is a sufficient number of bathrooms en route.

That's what late pregnancy all boils down to—proximity to a bathroom.

Traveling with a two-and-a-half-year-old takes your mind off bathrooms—at least for a while. When the tape player in our Subaru broke (what happened, actually, was that "A Grouch's Christmas" became digested in the depths of the tape player's guts), we panicked. Our anxiety increased when the Subaru fix-it people couldn't fix it until after Christmas. That meant sixteen hours in the car without a tape player to entertain Courtney.

Horrors!

Thank goodness for the advent of tape recorders, which I think came before tape players. So right now, we're listening to a story about Big Bird getting a new puppy named Barkley. Everybody on Sesame Street from Sherlock Hemlock to Prairie Dawn is giving Big Bird advice on how to raise this dog. Because this is a fascinating storyline, my attention is temporarily not on bathrooms.

Naturally, when the Sesame Street gang starts to give Big Bird pointers on potty training Barkley, I start to think about two things:

.

1) How I can apply some of this wisdom to potty training Courtney?

2) How many bathrooms there are between here and Nashville?

DAY 199

It's Christmas. It's the last Christmas when there will be just the three of us.

I don't know. I kind of feel like this little person inside me is just as much a big part of the holidays this year as if he/she were already born.

Of course, he/she certainly is easier to take care of than he/she will be next Christmas.

DAY 200

It's time for my annual Post-Christmas Letdown.

That's a term I learned from "Peanuts." I think Lucy was stricken with it. See? This is yet another fine example of the many benefits found in reading. Reading is fundamental.

Still, the after-Christmas blues can be depressing, but I guess that's what they're supposed to be. Otherwise, they wouldn't be called the blues.

The other "blues" that hit me—and hit me harder than those after the holidays—are the Post-Partum Blues. I'm already dreading the onset of this depression that typically hits a few days after delivery.

I remember crying after being overwhelmed with grief when the hospital told me I'd be checking out on Thursday. Why Thursday?! Why not Friday? Or Wednesday? Those were much better days to check out and bring the baby home than on a crummy ol' Thursday.

The hospital refused to listen to hormonal reasoning.

DAY 201

I'm doing my part to prevent the spread of varicose veins. I've stopped crossing my legs.

Of course, I couldn't cross my legs even if I wanted to, which is fine because I don't want to because I can't.

Besides, it would give me varicose veins.

I'm not sure what varicose veins are, anyhow. It's just that since I was three years old, I've been instilled with the notion that having varicose veins is a bad thing.

Like crow's feet.

You know, those lines that protrude from the corners of your eyes, resembling out-of-place eyelashes. I think you get them when you smile too much.

So what's a happy person who wants to cross her legs (assuming she's not seven-and-a-half months pregnant and can still do so) to do?

It doesn't matter, because at this late stage of pregnancy, it's difficult enough to find reasons to smile until after the baby's born, and as I mentioned earlier, it's even more difficult to cross your legs.

So stop worrying about such trivial things and focus more on ways to get rid of the newfound fat that's taken over your thighs, or what to do with the unsightly stretch marks that are creeping up your tummy.

Serious stuff like that.

DAY 202

Today is our seventh wedding anniversary.

Being married for seven years sure sounds like a long time, especially when you're spending the day in the back seat of a Subaru wagon with your two-and-a-half-year-old when you're suffering from a strength-draining stomach virus as you, your husband, and your daughter make the eight-hour trek back home after the holidays.

Whew.

We are getting older. And more domesticated, too, pushing romance aside for little things like the getting-back-to-work-on-time-so-you-won't-lose-your-job chore.

Of course, as a very pregnant woman pushing her thirtieth pound, I fret about the famous "Seven-Year Itch." My worries are unfounded as long as I remember that Bryan is indeed attracted to very pregnant women with stomach viruses.

DAY 203

There are so many things in this world I don't understand.

Like that commercial about some Colombian coffee, "…hand-picked by Juan Valdez."

That's got to be one busy guy!

It would be hard enough for him to pick the beans just for his own coffee, but he obviously does it for everybody who drinks that brand.

I also don't understand why they call that game show the *$100,000 Pyramid*. Whenever I've seen contestants win in the lightning round or whatever it's called, they win only $2,500, never $100,000. I guess it's the $100,000 pyramid to those few-and-far-between contestants who win a total of $97,500 after a jillion rounds and then win again.

Or what about the little boy who arranges to drop in on neighbors at precisely the exact time they're sitting down to a hot meal of Stove-Top stuffing.

I just don't understand why his own mom doesn't fix it.

DAY 204

I haven't read this anywhere in the pregnancy books yet, but I'm sure a woman's toenails grow faster when she's pregnant than when she's not.

Okay, maybe it just seems that way because it takes the length of time it takes to grow them to cut them because she can't reach them.

Does that make sense?

To the nonpregnant person, no. To me and thousands of other pregnant women, a strong yes!

Just putting on a good pair of socks (see earlier entry that defines what good socks are when you're pregnant) can be an all-night experience. That's why I try to keep them clean and free of odor once I do have them on to curtail the number of times I have to change them.

Then, add the complexities of cutting your toenails, and

there's hardly any time left to count the number of stretch marks that have appeared on your girth. I keep a calculator handy to make this chore more time-efficient.

DAY 205

The onset of the new year has spurred me to do something I've been meaning to do for several months.

Order birth announcements.

Of course, since we don't know if the baby is a boy or a girl and since we don't know what we'll end up naming him or her and since we don't know how big the baby will be and since we don't know when the baby will be born, the announcements won't be engraved.

I prefer the personal touch: filling in the blanks myself. Which means I also prefer the economical touch.

We're going with a golf theme this time around. Courtney's announcement had a tennis theme. The cards have appropriate expressions describing the baby, i.e., "Teed off on..." instead of born on. That sort of thing.

Okay, so we're going for the cute-birth-announcement theme.

DAY 206

Speaking of golf, I kicked off 1993 with a fabulous round— for me, that is.

I beat my father-in-law by a stroke and lost to Bryan only by two strokes. (However, my father-in-law discarded the score card, so I'm sure he'll deny the whole thing.) They grumbled about how badly they played; I kept quiet and silently enjoyed how well I did play.

But I'm paying for it now.

I hadn't played golf since we went to the beach four months ago, and some important golf muscles had been put away for the season—or buried beneath mounds of fat from the thirty pounds I've gained. So now these important golf muscles are sore.

Plus, I really hadn't considered the effort it takes to swing a golf club. Maybe if I had, my score would've been even better.

Yet, it seems to me that in addition to lifting and swinging a driver during a typical tee shot, I also must lift and swing about twenty pounds of upper-torso weight. Tally all that weight, and it feels like I'm swinging a sledgehammer.

Which explains why I outdrove Bryan a time or two.

DAY 207

Whoever invented the word "sluggish" was thinking about a woman after seven-and-a-half months of pregnancy. Indeed, Mr. Webster even included a drawing of one such woman to further define "sluggish."

Or was it "slug?"

Sometimes I feel sluggish, and other times I feel like a slug. Bryan recalls that I seemed to feel perkier when I was pregnant with Courtney this far along. His theory is that keeping up with Courtney is why I feel so run down this time around.

Perhaps.

Today we both worked out at the "Y." Bryan's on an I-Ate-Too-Much-Over-The-Holidays-And-The-Preceding-Sixteen-Months-So-Now-I-Need-To-Lose-Fifteen-Pounds-Before-I-Turn-Thirty-In-Two-Months Diet.

Talk about nerve.

Of course, he announces this on the very day I hit the thirty-pound mark. Why can't he wait a mere six weeks or so when this baby is born so I can join him? *I'm* the one who really needs to lose it—not him. He looks great.

I look "great," too, only in a different sense. Mr. Webster definitely had me in mind when he came up with definition #1 for "great (grat), adj. (A.S.) that means absolutely spacious: 1) of much more than ordinary size, extent, volume, etc., as in The Great Lakes."

There's nothing for getting you out of a sluggish mood like having yourself compared directly with five large bodies of fresh water that border the United States and Canada.

DAY 208

About that workout yesterday…I just don't know if I'll be

able to reach my goal of working out until labor sets in. One simple solution, it might be suggested, is to reduce the intensity and activity of my workouts.

I've already done that.

I'm down to a thirty-minute walk around the track every now and then. More then than now, but I'm trying to go to the "Y" more. Note I didn't say "brisk" walk. It's difficult to be brisk with a 30-pound weight strapped around you. And it's not like after the walk you get to detach the Velcro and skip to the showers.

I have made one stride, however. I no longer compare my workout with those of the sleek, Spandex-clad girls who couldn't grow a stretch mark if they tried. I realize my station in life right now. I admit it's taken me seven-and-a-half months, but I now am content to compare me with me.

Except for that guy I shared the track with yesterday who looked like he was fifteen months along. I boasted to myself, "Hey, I can outwalk him. I can even outwalk him briskly." But, to my dismay, he walked full circles around me within five laps or so. I tried to keep ahead, but my body wouldn't do what I wanted it to. His obviously did.

I've got to realize my limitations.

DAY 209

I got a part-time job today.

I have mixed emotions about it, though.

Not about the job—I think that's fine. I'll be working for an AM radio station on weeknights and weekends. It'll do me good to get out of the house every so often and bring in a few extra bucks.

The mixed emotions stem from the program director's reaction to my pregnancy. When he asked me when I could start, I and my extra thirty-two pounds responded, "You know I'm pregnant, don't you?"

"No."

But then he quickly added that it was fine that I was pregnant and that there would be no heavy lifting. (I think the Equal

Opportunity Employment people had the interviewing room bugged.)

"I mean I'm very pregnant. I'm due in five or six weeks."

"Oh."

Again he said this wasn't a problem and told me when I had the baby not to come back to work until I was ready and feeling fine.

I was impressed by that last remark, coming from someone who respects my work before I even start to work. But that does not overshadow the fact that nonpregnant folks in the outside world do not see me as seven-and-a-half months pregnant.

I guess they see me as fat.

It's time I get respect for being pregnant.

DAY 210

I should be a poster child for the cold and flu season.

Once again—and for the second time in a month—I've come down with a cold. I think Courtney's coming down with one, too.

But this year I resolve not to complain about stuff like that. Oh, I'll mention it occasionally, but not complain about it. In fact, instead of wallowing around on the sofa today trying to breathe, I went to the "Y" to pursue my goal of working out until labor sets in.

I won't be surprised if my labor sets in while I'm on the track.

Eighth Month

DAY 211

I walked the track at the "Y" again today. Not a brisk walk, more like a brisk waddle.

But at least I'm sticking to my goal.

I remember when Bryan and I took a birthing class when I was pregnant with Courtney, they referred to the time of pregnancy as being in training. Much like a runner training for a race. Or a boxer training for a fight.

I must be raising a boxer in there. He/she punches me incessantly. Of course, he/she could be kicking me. So maybe I'm raising a kick boxer.

DAY 212

I've already discussed the advantages of having a soap opera baby—the kind that you rarely see on screen, and when they are, they're never wet, dirty, crying, colicky, cranky, etc. And they grow up much faster, sort of like dog years, so they could feasibly reach puberty by the time their off-screen counterparts reach potty-training.

(Which reminds me, if I don't get on the ball with Courtney, she may not be potty-trained until puberty.)

Anyway, I also pointed out the disadvantages of having this perfect baby who's out of diapers before we can change socks. Then there's the soap opera pregnant woman. These women never gain more than fifteen pounds, which accounts for why they never have weight to lose after they give birth. They never get stretch marks. They have the most dramatic birthing experiences, like when they're walking down the aisle to the beat of "The Wedding March." And their on-screen pregnancies last about three-and-a-half months.

I really can't think of any disadvantages to this type of pregnancy, except maybe the part about going into labor while you're getting married.

Well, today I saw something I just couldn't believe: The Soap Opera Home-Pregnancy-Test-Experience. In this totally unrealistic scene, this unmarried teenage girl who's living with this unmarried teenage guy goes to a drug store to buy "Know Now," a home pregnancy test for unmarried teenage girls on soap operas. While she's buying it, she runs into another unmarried teenage guy who used to date her but never lived with her or even slept with her. He catches her with "Know Now," and after she makes the purchase, they go to a fancy restaurant to talk about it. The whole time, she's wondering if she's pregnant, and she's wondering while she's got the test that could prove it in her purse. He's wondering, too, but they just sit and talk about how they're wondering about it. Then he tells her she must tell her unmarried teenage live-in boyfriend that she's wondering about it.

Doesn't anybody care how much these tests cost!?

When I got my test—at Wal-Mart with a coupon—I broke speed limits as I rushed home to find out. I recognized the value of these tests. True, I was a little shocked at the result and wanted a second opinion from my doctor in spite of the test's 99.9887854 percent accuracy rate. But at least I didn't sit and wonder about it.

If soap operas continue with this kind of fantasyland, then people are going to start disbelieving them.

DAY 213

As of today, I'm boycotting scales.

Including the weigh stations along the interstate.

At this point, it doesn't seem to matter what I eat, what I don't eat, what I would like to eat, what I wouldn't like to eat, I'm still going to gain weight.

And I'd prefer not to know about it.

This new attitude about my late-stage pregnancy weight makes it difficult to support Bryan's new attitude about his late-20s slow metabolism, which has sparked his resolution to lose weight in two months.

Of course, here I am, no longer caring about my weight, ironically on one of the most important nonholidays of the year.

Elvis's birthday.

In fact, today the skinny Elvis stamp went on sale. If you'll recall, Americans didn't want the fat Elvis on a commemorative stamp. They preferred to remember him as he was, not how he ended up.

That's exactly how I feel.

DAY 214

I'm enjoying a rare treat today.

I call it "Home Alone 34." The 34, of course, stands for thirty-four weeks along.

Bryan and Courtney are in Spartanburg visiting the Nutt side of the family, and I stayed behind in Salem basking in the peace and quiet.

The best part is I get to do whatever I want, whenever I want, and however I want. Bad movies, for example. I love bad movies. I'm probably the biggest *Grease 2* fan on earth. So this afternoon I watched a classic Valerie Bertinelli flick where she's this nun who's got the hots—or whatever you call it in nun terms—for this dorky-looking priest. It's not like it's believable or anything; I just can't see Mrs. Eddie Van Halen going after a priest, especially a dorky-looking one.

Then I got to eat Doritos. We have a rule in the Nutt House: No Dorito-eating if:

a) You're planning to kiss someone in the family within the next twenty-four hours.

b) You're planning to breathe near someone in the family within the next twenty-four hours.

c) You're planning to use the letter *h* in a word within the next twenty-four hours.

Forget trying to cover up the Dorito-causing halitosis with a tube of toothpaste. Yes, the whole tube. Dorito odor still prevails and lurks deep within the mouth, throat, and even lungs. It's a serious situation, but only when loved ones dare get too close.

But today, that wasn't my problem as there I was sitting around the house watching a bad movie and wallowing in bad breath.

Ecstasy.

DAY 215

Like those people who've won the Publisher's House Sweepstakes, I didn't think it would happen to me.

No, I didn't win the drawing. This is much more far-fetched than that.

I've outgrown a maternity dress.

Horrors.

Outgrowing a maternity dress is not an easy thing to do. You have to work at it—mainly by gaining a pound every two or three days like I've been doing lately.

I have a pair of snap-on maternity blue jeans I outgrew months ago. That's not so rare. A lot of maternity pants don't give the wearer much slack. No pun intended.

Okay, maybe I did stay up all night coming up with that one.

Plus, I broke the snap off one side of a pair of maternity jeans I was wearing at the time. I think I was eating a banana or something. They don't make maternity jeans like they used to.

And they certainly don't make maternity dresses like they used to, either. This was my favorite maternity dress, if there can be such a thing. It wasn't one of those Christmas-tree-shaped jumpers that looks like a moo-moo. I don't mean those fashionable dresses in Hawaii worn by guests on the old *Don Ho Show*. I mean a cow.

Actually, it was a cute blue-and-white pin-striped (for a thinning effect) pullover jumper that, for some reason I don't know except maybe it was designed by a man, gathered just below the hip and then flared back out. Kind of like a flapper dress without the fringes, which I've always thought looked like a drape. That's not to criticize drapes; Vivien Leigh wore one in *Gone with the Wind* and looked just splendid.

Anyway, with the amount of weight I'm gaining in the home stretch mark, I'd probably be better off wearing window dressings.

DAY 216

The baby has been particularly active today.

And particularly painful.

But it's all a part of late-stage pregnancy and simply adds to my desire for the next month and two days to hurry up. I try not to think that way, however, because I believe it's wrong to wish your life away like that.

Besides that, I just might get my wish and have this baby before I'm ready.

I did a lot of "nesting" this past weekend. Chores which included buying bottles and boiling nipples, buying formula, and preparing a proper storage place for the above, and mopping.

Mopping?

I've mopped even when I haven't been pregnant—only when the Board of Health threatens. I don't enjoy mopping.

I'd seek counseling if I did.

And come to think of it, it really doesn't make much sense why I'd get this maternal urge to mop my kitchen floor when it's most likely going to get dirty again way before this baby will be on it.

DAY 217

Braxton Hicks.

First of all, who would name their child *Braxton*. Second, I don't understand why false labor pains are named after him.

Not her. *Him*.

I've heard it's because he's the one who first discovered them.

Wrong.

The mom-to-be who had them had to be the first one to discover them.

But it's a man's world, even in the world of pregnancy.

Anyway, I've had a lot of these male-named uterine contractions lately. It seems I've had more of them this time than with Courtney. Maybe I'm just more aware of them now that I'm at home with this pregnancy.

Braxton Nutt. (Braxtonia if it's a girl.)

Nawww.

DAY 218

The countdown has started again.

I'm due in one month, which is usually more time than they give you for a library book.

However, my due date's not renewable.

I suppose I could be overdue for a week or two without paying late charges. Any further along than that, they'll probably induce.

I'd rather pay the fine. Inducing labor doesn't appeal to me at all. And I don't see how it would appeal to the baby, either— being forcibly evicted from the only home he or she has ever known.

Not a good way to be introduced to this world.

But medically speaking from a person who's not medically inclined at all, I guess they don't want mom to give birth to something the size of a porpoise.

Not a good way to be introduced to motherhood.

DAY 219

With less than a month to go on this gestation period, I've diversified my workout a little bit, just for diversification's sake. And because I'm getting bored with the thirty-minute brisk waddle. Doesn't Jane Fonda have a videotape for that workout?

Today, I shot baskets for a few minutes before beginning my waddle.

The first thing I discovered is that a pregnant woman in her eighth month must dribble farther away from her body than what she's accustomed to doing. Second, that same aforementioned woman can't chase after the ball as quickly as she once could, allowing the ball to roll all the way to the other end of the court. And last, I learned my limits as to how far out I can shoot the ball and reach the basket because...

Pregnant Women Can't Jump.

The foul line, I found out, is my limit. Any farther away, I'm shooting an air ball. In a nonpregnant state, I have to jump to shoot the ball from long distances. I wouldn't necessarily call it a jump shot, although that does sound classy and sound like I'm some sort of basketball star. I prefer to call a spade a spade and call this type of shot an Umph Shot. My jump gives it that extra "umph" to make it to the goal.

I've always had a good Umph Shot. Growing up, I was the envy of every girl in my neighborhood who was also trying to perfect the Umph Shot. I should mention there were just three girls, including myself, in my neighborhood, and one of the other two had no interest in basketball.

My Umph Shot has won me many a horse game, including some against my own husband. He and I played horse a few times within forty-eight hours before Courtney was born.

I remember winning twice. I don't know if Bryan let me win.

That's not his style. I do know at that time I couldn't rely on my Umph Shot to push me into victory.

I had to save my Umphs for the big event two days later.

DAY 220

There are just some places an eight-month-pregnant woman has no business being in.

That playground thing filled with colorful plastic balls at your favorite fast-food restaurant is a good example, especially if the reason for the eight-month-pregnant woman being in it is to fetch her two-and-a-half-year-old. It's one of those things you put your kid in while you munch away on a quarter-pounder and other fast food items in peace. That is, until the kid wants out and isn't big enough to get out on his/her own.

Anyway, halfway in, I was stopped by my friend, Judy, who's been eight months pregnant twice. She knew instinctively that the ball playground was not the place for me.

Whew.

DAY 221

Even though I no longer care about the amount of weight I've gained, I feel compelled to record it here anyway.

Thirty-four pounds.

In the immortal words of Charlie Brown, who's never been eight months pregnant, "Aaaaauuurgggghhh!!!!"

I didn't say I don't occasionally experience a momentary loss of control when I realize how much I've gained; I merely said I don't care. I also don't care if I momentarily lose control. These conflicting emotions are controlled by different parts of the brain. Obviously, there's been a failure in communication, a memo that's been shredded.

But I've been thinking on the bright side of things. It could've been thirty-five pounds. Of course, it could've been thirty-three pounds had I bypassed that extra slice of red velvet cake at Christmas.

There's another bright side. I could've been carrying all this extra weight all along. But weight gain during pregnancy is gradual so you can get used to the extra weight a little at a time.

Of course, the flip side is that pregnancy weight sneaks up on you too fast.

DAY 222

Here I sit in drag. Or is it "in draggette"?

Because our dryer has been shrinking my clothes, my maternity wardrobe has been shrinking as well. But, on the bright side, if there comes a flood—say, the Roanoke River jumps its banks—and I'm wearing my pink sweat pants, (which when stretched to the limit reveal my sexy, eight-month-pregnant, water-retaining calves), then I don't have a worry in the world.

So for those days when massive river flooding is not an immediate threat, I have chosen to wear my husband's clothes. Call it cross-dressing, which is appropriate because Bryan gets cross when I wear his clothes.

I don't think he's too happy about my wearing his dress shirts, which I button halfway down and wear something maternally sporty over it. I was wearing my own button-down shirts, but I'm down to buttoning only the top button so it's necessary to wear Bryan's.

I firmly believe a lot of this can be attributed to water retention. Today I've had to take off my wedding rings and wear them on a gold chain—all due to water retention.

Okay, so I'm bloated.

DAY 223

If I read my calendar correctly, today—Martin Luther King, Jr.'s Birthday Observed—is the last major holiday before my baby is due.

I don't think Groundhog Day counts.

I guess it does if you're a groundhog, though.

Since my due date is a day before Valentine's Day, there's always the chance he/she could pick that day to be born. If he/she thinks it through, though, he/she would probably want to wait at least until the fifteenth.

Why? It's the same reason people born on or around Christmas wish they weren't: they get cheated out of presents. Like the kid opens up a Tonka truck from Aunt Grace (everybody has an Aunt Grace), and he's all excited about it (the Tonka truck, not the fact that everyone has an Aunt Grace). Christmas spirit fills his little impressionable heart until Aunt Grace says, "It's your birthday present, too."

What a blow.

I know a little bit about the problem because I was born two days after St. Patrick's Day, which means my St. Patrick's Day gifts are practically cut in half. It's a thorn in my side I've learned to live with.

Same thing with being born near Valentine's Day. Loved ones would be too cheap to give two presents or two cards or two whatevers.

Nobody said life was fair.

DAY 224

It's a snowy day outside, and I'm inside making potty deals with Courtney.

Things like, "You can watch a *Barney* video if you do such and such on the potty."

I need to get outside in the snow more.

Actually, I don't call it "such and such"; I'd just prefer not to get graphic here. Bryan and I really haven't agreed on what to call it anyway. (If we can't agree on something like this, it's no wonder we can't agree on the baby's name!)

We do agree we don't like what Courtney calls one of them—again, I won't mention what in this space—but we have to go along with it because a friend of ours who was potty-training her daughter months ago inadvertently sold Courtney on the term.

Still, that leaves what to call the other one open. What we're calling it now is Bryan's idea, but I use the same word in so many other contexts, I'm afraid Courtney will become confused.

She probably already is because she hasn't done it yet.

That's why I'm making deals with her on this snowy day.

DAY 225

The vital statistics are in.

I've gained thirty-five pounds and dilated about one centimeter.

Yikes.

I knew there would come a time when weight mattered nothing to me, and the time has come. The dilation and thinning of the cervix has taken its place.

It means the time is near.

The doctor told me not to get over-anxious about it—just like he did months ago about my rapid weight gain. He doubted I'd go into labor within a week, but then again he didn't rule out two weeks. And then again, I may go another month.

Still, this dilation business really makes it seem around the corner—a lot more so than counting the days on the calendar. It makes it seem more real, like it's really going to happen.

So I've been spending the day inhaling all of that.

DAY 226

Bryan's body is almost as serious about losing weight as mine is about gaining it.

Today, there are just seven pounds separating us. Seven pounds between Bryan and his personal achievement. (He would love to say that I weigh more than he does.) Seven pounds between me and embarrassment. (I would love for him not to.)

Unless I go into labor in the next three days, which I doubt will happen, I will probably surpass my TWG (Total Weight Gain) that I had with Courtney, which was thirty-six pounds. To gain seven in the next three-and-a-half weeks would mean a lot of Sara Lee goodies.

What worries me about this Bryan-losing-weight thing is that Bryan refuses to touch Sara Lee. While I admire his loyalty to me—even in these deep dark days of convex stomachs, thunder thighs and pudgy ankles—I still would like for him to give in to his primal urges and have a few slices of the coconut cake I bought last week.

Mainly because as I see it vanish from the plate, I have to accept that I've been the only one consuming all those nagging calories I'll have to deal with after I give birth. (Well, I have had about seventy-three calories' worth of help from Courtney.)

Bryan prefers to eat a ripe banana to quell his longing for sweets.

This lady prefers Sara Lee.

DAY 227

I have some new concerns now that my due date seems to be quickly approaching. Here are a few:

• Bryan has informed me that he has to take two business trips between now and then. Should we teach Courtney how to be an effective, supportive labor coach in case the big day comes while he's gone? "Breathe, Mommy, breathe!"

• The dilation has begun. Who knows, I may have been dilated since conception because that's not something you normally go around checking. However, I read that in the first phase of the first stage of labor mom may not have dilated even a centimeter. I'm already about a centimeter, so I'm definitely ahead of my time.

• Who is going to watch Courtney while I'm in the hospital (assuming, of course, I don't have to use her as my labor coach)? I probably should quit pondering and start asking some friends.

• I must avoid having this baby on Superbowl Sunday in nine days. Dallas—Bryan's favorite team—is playing. Well, there's always Courtney to help me out.

• What if my water breaks while I'm on the track in the gym at the "Y"?

I think I was better off when my biggest concern was my weight gain.

DAY 228

Three weeks!

I'm really proud of myself. With my workout days surely

numbered, I am still working toward my goal…in spite of those annoying aerobics people.

It's Saturday, and there was a bunch of annoying aerobics people hogging up the gym where Bryan and I were going to play a grudge game of horse. So we punted the horse idea and decided to do separate workouts. However, my workout of thirty minutes of brisk walking on the track in the gym meant that I had to be in the company of these annoying aerobics people.

Here are a few reasons why I find them annoying:

• They play annoying, never-heard-before music at a zillion decibels, drowning out my cool, brisk-walking tunes blasting through the earphones of my Brisk Walkman.

• They look annoying, especially the guys, and especially the guys sporting tube socks and Keds. And there are some guys who have no business wearing Spandex.

• They make annoying sounds, shouting annoying words for no apparent reason, like "Yeah!" and "Whooooooaaaaaa!"

Maybe it wouldn't be so bad if my water breaks while I'm briskly walking on the track above them.

DAY 229

The doctor told me this baby is smaller than Courtney was, which therefore increases the likelihood of a VBAC—Vaginal Birth After Cesarean.

Which also means I'm reading again.

Reading about VBACs and labor in general. For the last eight months or so, I thought I'd simply have another C-section—maybe even scheduled—and wouldn't have to worry about how to time contractions, how to know when to start pushing, how to breathe.

It's my lay–pregnant woman's understanding that insurance companies have gotten huffy about too many unnecessary C-sections, creating profitable conditions for the physician and hospital. I have confidence that my OB/GYN group is conservative on this issue and performs them only when conditions warrant.

That's comforting.

What's not so comforting is the fear of the unknown, the doctor told me. At least I know what to expect with a C-section, even though it hurts more and the recovery time is longer.

So by reading and refreshing my memory of the stuff I learned in birthing classes three years ago, I'm conquering this fear.

DAY 230

Just when I thought Bryan and I had come to some sort of an agreement—okay, a compromise—on baby names, we really haven't come to a compromise.

I do think we've decided on a boy's name. It's the girl's name that's giving us trouble again. Our new compromise called for Bryan to choose the girl's first name and I, the middle name, and for me to choose the boy's first name and Bryan, the middle.

Sounded fair at the time.

Call me touchy, but Bryan didn't like my choice of the girl's middle name. I felt that was in direct violation of our compromise, so I gave the Allied Forces a call. They weren't home, so I retaliated with my own violation.

I no longer liked his choice for the girl's first name.

Sounds fair now.

It does concern me as we're two weeks and five days away from my due date, a date that feasibly could occur in much less time than that. But panic hasn't quite set in yet.

After all, it took several episodes for Murphy Brown to name her son—*after* he was born, incidentally.

DAY 231

You know you're getting late in your pregnancy when:

• Terry cloth socks cut off the circulation to your ankles.

• The stretch marks on your stomach resemble a map tracing several routes from Baton Rouge, Louisiana to Lansing, Michigan.

• There is no such thing as a bathroom that is close enough for you.

• You use your tummy as a prop when you write checks to the grocery store.

• You begin to look at the "before" photos of those women in weight-loss-program commercials and think, "Boy, if I only had *her* figure!"

• You have your own reserved parking place at the OB/GYN's.

• Sitting, standing, sleeping, and breathing are now at the core of your workout program.

• The scale flinches when it sees you coming.

• You come up with creative ways to shave your legs.

• You and/or your husband decide after all this time you don't like the names you've chosen for the baby.

• You begin to feel empathy for the beached whales on old *Jacques Cousteau* reruns.

• Water retention forces you to take off your wedding rings.

• You've been preadmitted to the hospital and packed your and the baby's stuff in a suitcase, except you realize most of the stuff that you've packed you're still using.

• And finally, YOU CAN'T WAIT TO HAVE THE BABY!

DAY 232

Today Bryan is on one of his business trips he had to take just before the baby is born.

Today I've been wondering if I'll know when it's time to go to the hospital.

I need Bryan to tell me.

Sounds strange? Not really. Remember, he was the one who told me I was pregnant in the first place.

After all, he does have a master's degree. So what if it's in engineering.

I don't care if other mothers forget what labor feels like. I certainly remember. Well, I remember the intense labor pains, and I remember begging for the epidural guy to relieve the agony. But I don't remember the prelabor stuff, and I'm afraid

I won't be able to differentiate between real labor and the normal aches and pains I have had on a daily basis recently. The only reason I knew before when to go to the hospital was my water broke.

And there's no mistaking that!

DAY 233

Results from my weekly examination today:
- Topped off at thirty-six pounds
- Measured in at one to two centimeters
- Registered normal in various lab tests

I didn't see my regular doctor today because I have to see each one in the practice at least once, because any one of them could have the privilege of assisting in the birth of my child. Which reminds me, why do they call it a "practice"? That's not a comforting term. I want to make sure they've got it down pat before they go birthing my child.

Anyway, it was a brief visit, briefer than the hour or so I waited with a two-and-a-half-year-old on PMS (Pre-Meal Syndrome). Of course, an hour with a two-and-a-half-year-old equates to seven by-yourself adult hours.

The doctor and I discussed the decrease in fetal movement and the increase of fetal hiccups—both of which are normal—but she wants me to monitor the movements more closely and if it concerns me, to come in for tests.

I think the baby is simply bored in there.

DAY 234

I haven't recorded a potty update recently. Here it is.

The potty itself is in pretty good shape, and it's proven to be quite durable these last few weeks as we've tried to coerce Courtney to *totally* flee the diaper scene before this baby arrives.

A part of her wants to linger there.

However, progress has been made, and I firmly believe her diaper days are about over. That's due to the advent of Pull-Ups, those disposable training pants that cost more than diapers and make her feel like a big kid now.

Keeping Courtney in diapers would have been the cheaper route at this point, but I'm glad she feels like a big kid now.

DAY 235

I woke up with Opie hair this morning.

I don't think it has anything to do with being pregnant, like some sort of Opie hormone that creeps into the female body once she conceives and then takes total control of her hair. (Of course, I'm talking about the Opie on *The Andy Griffith Show*. What other Opie is there?) I think it has to do with my bangs simply getting too long to brush back. So what happens is through the course of nature, my bangs fall over my fore-head—which comes in handy when I've got a pimple there—and the end product is that I look like Opie.

Sometimes, however, I have Beaver hair.

Again, there haven't been enough scientific studies in the gynecological field to determine if Beaver hair is pregnancy-related, and I tend to agree with whatever gynecological experts come up with when it comes to hairstyles and pregnancy. So that settles that.

What I'm referring to here is Beaver Cleaver hair—you know, from *Leave It to Beaver*. In my case, it's caused by not having enough time to go to the beauty salon to get my bangs trimmed. Or by not wanting to spend $15 for someone at the beauty salon to trim my bangs. Usually it's the latter—I'm not really all that busy. So what I do to save the megabucks in order to send Courtney and my unborn to college is trim my own bangs. I have a bachelor's degree in journalism and a pair of scissors, so I figure, "Why not?"

Because I end up with forty-five-degree angle bangs.

DAY 236

It's Superbowl Sunday, and I've been instructed not to give birth today.

A small request, I suppose.

For one thing, we're hosting a Superbowl party at our house

for twenty or so people tonight. They've made their plans. I can't disappoint them and tell them they'd have to watch the big game in the maternity floor lounge.

But as I said earlier, Dallas is playing. Dallas is Bryan's favorite team. Bryan's not simply a fair-weather fan, supporting them only when they have a winning season or make it to the Superbowl. Nope. Bryan liked Dallas when liking Dallas wasn't cool. Bryan takes it seriously; his palms break out in a sweaty dew when he watches them play.

I used to be able to do that to him.

Of course, right now I look like the woman who just swallowed the football, so it's hard to achieve that effect on my husband.

DAY 237

I feel like a bomb.

A forty-pound bomb.

I'm no psychic. And I don't know Dionne Warwick personally. Regardless, there are no psychics—just lucky guessers. But I'll offer up this guess: I'm going to have this baby this month, based on my due date, which is a mere twelve days away.

T minus twelve and counting.

Well, seemingly everyone who desires to strike up a conversation with me now bypasses the usual salutations, greetings, how-do-you-do's, etc. and instead asks, "How much longer you got to go?" They don't even bother to use proper grammar.

Or they get more personal: "Have you dilated yet?" Others ask me for the umpteenth time, "When are you due?" I guess they haven't bothered to read the ad I took out on the public access channel—Karen Nutt Is Due To Give Birth February 13, 1993. Quit Asking Her!

Then, there are the comments.

"You look like you're ready to have that baby." (Those were the precise words of a teenage guy who's a cashier at Kroger and whom I'd never met before.)

"I can tell by the way you're carrying, you're going to have a boy/girl." (Like they really know.)

"My, you're getting big." (My personal favorite.)

About this forty-pound thing…if you've been charting my weight, you know I weighed in at thirty-six pounds just four days ago. Do you realize what you have to eat to gain that much in four days?

There must be some mistake.

DAY 238

Yes, there has been some mistake with the alleged four-pound weight gain.

It's only three pounds.

At least that's what my scales tell me this morning. They don't say much, actually. In the last few months, all they've been able to utter is "Ouch!"

Nevertheless, today is Groundhog Day. Not to be confused with Veterans' Day, Secretary's Day, or Mothers-in-Law Day, you don't have to do anything special for your favorite groundhog. It's a holiday that focuses on one groundhog and his one shadow, or lack of it. The next six weeks of winter hang in the balance.

February 2 also used to be my due date.

DAY 239

Well, I didn't have this baby on my original due date. Who'd want to share the spotlight with a groundhog anyway?

I did go to my weekly doctor's visit yesterday. The most up-to-date stats are as follows:

•Gained thirty-nine pounds

•Measured in at one to two centimeters

•Effaced seventy-five percent

It's that last stat that's scary. I don't like to think about how much I've effaced. I'm not even sure what it means.

Simply speaking, I think it means the odds are greater that my water will break while I'm on the track at the "Y." I hope it's during aerobics class.

DAY 240

I can see the light at the end of the tunnel just as this baby can see the light at the end of the vagina.

A crude simile, I suppose.

But I'm simply trying to convey that the time is drawing nigh for this baby to enter the world. He or she will soon have to get used to a new diet. In a few days, he or she must give up a hearty diet of bologna and cheese sandwiches, barbecue chips, Nilla Wafers, Monday-night spaghetti, late-night bowls of Cap'n Crunch Berries cereal, and an occasional $1.99 chopped steak at Western Sizzlin' in favor of more nourishing bottles of formula.

(Unfortunately, I'll probably have to give up the same in favor of losing all the postpartum weight.)

Ninth Month

DAY 241

Today the mailman delivered the first newsletter focusing on life with the new baby.

I haven't had the new baby yet.

Besides, I know what life is like with a new baby. My curiosity, therefore, now focuses more on life with the new baby *and* toddler. I guess I'll have to find out on my own. Bryan will also find out—after all, he got me into this to begin with.

Anyway, this newsletter is yet another reminder that it won't be long. I predict I'll have this new baby on February eighth. That's a Monday. That's also my doctor's on-call day. I really want him to deliver the new baby, so I'm going to meditate real hard on it on Monday.

The practice labor pains seem to be more frequent the last

few days. So much so that I get a little nervous when I leave home, especially now when I'm at work…at the radio station, not exactly the best place to leave at the spur of the moment. Or, more metaphorically, at the first drop upon my water breaking.

I hope not; I'm saving that for those annoying aerobics people below the track at the "Y."

DAY 242

One week away!

From a selfish standpoint, there are so many things I look forward to soon after the baby is born. Here's a brief list:

• Becoming reacquainted with my toes
• Having a ceremonial burning of my maternity underwear
• Doing a belly flop
• Getting a perm and a new 'do
• Crossing my legs
• Sitting on the floor without worrying whether I'll be able to get up
• Wearing clothes designed specifically for women with *waists*
• Taking a long, hot, Calgon bath
• Playing tennis
• Losing weight!!!
• Riding a horse

Actually, I never understood why a pregnant woman shouldn't ride a horse. Too much weight on the horse? If so, then a fat woman shouldn't ride a horse. Or maybe it's the bumping motion, which might cause early labor. I don't know.

Anyway, I'm ready to have this baby…and to get back in the saddle again.

DAY 243

My maternal instincts are kicking in—it won't be long now.

DAY 244

Okay, so I predicted wrong.
I didn't have this baby yesterday.

I *wanted* to have this baby yesterday. I'm big, I'm tired, I'm bloated, I'm cranky…

Sounds an awful lot like PMS.

That's one thing that bugs me, when people come up and tell me that because I'm pregnant, I don't have to worry about periods for nine months.

Yeah, right.

Periods don't go away. Never. They take a leave of absence during pregnancy and make up for nine months of lost time for weeks following birth.

And you have to put up with this period while you're caring for a new baby, and in my case a new baby and a toddler.

I will make one more prediction—and I'm sure I'll be right with this one: with all the chaos that'll be going on during this upcoming period, what with the new baby and the toddler, I will look forward to having my *monthly* periods from now on.

DAY 245

The time is drawing closer.

Of course, the time has been drawing closer since this pregnancy began nearly nine months ago.

But now it's *really* close.

Speaking of time, it's close to four in the afternoon, so it's not too late to have this baby today, birthday of William Henry Harrison.

Who in the world is William Henry Harrison, many nonstudents of American history ask. He's probably the one president (he's the ninth) historians have trouble criticizing. That's because he served just one month. He died of pneumonia after delivering a lengthy inauguration speech in the chilly January weather. He's also the grandfather of Benjamin Harrison, our twenty-third president.

Today is also my brother's birthday. He sells computer stuff, would look funny wearing a top hat while giving an inauguration speech, and is not old enough to be a grandfather.

I suppose there are others born today, but time is running out if this baby is to be among them.

DAY 246

I thought for sure last night I would to go into labor.

I was wrong.

I am very eager to have this baby—for my sake and the baby's, but I must keep in mind it's going to happen when God says it's time to.

And last night wasn't the time.

At my most recent doctor's visit two days ago, I had

• Gained forty-two pounds (I'm on the Three-Pound-A-Week plan.)

• Measured the same, at one to two centimeters (I was disappointed at that one.)

• Effaced 80-90 percent (I still don't know what it means, except that it's getting close.)

My doctor told me to go ahead and make an appointment for next week, but he doubted very seriously if I'll have to keep it.

Which means he gives me a week.

Today is the second full day of that week, and as of four in the afternoon, it's still the second full day of that week. Today is also the day Bryan predicted I would have this baby.

He could still be right, but I doubt it. I firmly believe I will not go into labor during the day. It'll be a night thing, just like when my labor began with Courtney. It's not normal to go into labor at four in the afternoon, since that's so close to when I have to start dinner. No, I don't have to worry about going into labor again until after midnight tomorrow, a good eight hours away.

I'm glad I have such a punctual womb.

DAY 247

I'm not necessarily saying Raymond Burr and Desi Arnaz, Sr. were the same person, but did you ever see them in the same room together?

Yes, my mind is going off on tangents, meaning that it's time to have this baby so I can concentrate on more important things.

Like, what is Kenny G's last name? Is it something he's ashamed of? Certainly, it can't be as bad as Nutt. That reminds me of the guy who played the neighbor on *Too Close for Comfort*, Jm. Bullock. Does that guy have something against vowels? And back to Kenny G...doesn't he look a lot like Darlene on *Roseanne*? You never see Kenny G and Darlene in the same room together, either.

There have been some physical developments that lead me to believe that I can soon start worrying about stuff like that. For three-and-a-half hours last night I experienced fairly regular contractions (five to ten minutes apart).

Then there was another physical development that I won't go into because it's kind of gross, but believe me, I was awfully close to calling the hospital and telling them about this gross development to see if it was time. (This gross development is quite natural, according to the doctor and the pregnancy books; I just don't want to discuss it in print, that's all.)

But the contractions seemed to wane during the night, although the gross development continued to develop. Nevertheless, I dismissed the idea of going to the hospital.

The contractions have been fewer and farther apart today. That's because it's *today*, not *tonight*. Contractions like the nighttime better because they seem a lot worse then to the mom-to-be.

I might have a daytime baby, but the labor will begin at night. You can quote me on that.

Unless I'm wrong.

DAY 248

Today I lost seven pounds and twelve-and-a-half ounces. At least.

IT'S A BOY! Weighing in at the aforementioned weight and measuring a lengthy twenty-one inches, Kyle McMillan Nutt entered the world at 4:07 A.M. Not exactly the most convenient time of day, but I didn't have plans for then anyway. Except maybe sleep.

Who would have thought it? It certainly didn't feel like I was going to have this baby today. The calm before the storm, I guess.

Here's what happened (All times are eastern standard time):

9:08 P.M. (Thursday night, seven hours before Kyle was born)—I hang up the phone after telling Mom I thought it would be a few more days.

9:24 P.M.—Water breaks while playing Legos with Courtney. I rush to the bathroom and do not get to see how *Cheers* ends.

9:31 P.M.—Bryan and I discuss whether "it's time."

9:33 P.M.—We think it is, so I call my good friend on standby to watch Courtney to tell her to stand by because we might be going to the hospital.

9:35 P.M.—I call the hospital and talk to the doctor on call to see if "it's time." She thinks it is.

9:38 P.M.—Bryan calls my good friend on standby to tell her "it's time."

9:43 P.M.—My brother in Dallas calls (it's 8:43 P.M. central standard time there) to chat. Bryan tells him we're on our way to the hospital. He and my sister-in-law say, quoting now, "Cool!"

9:50 P.M.—My good friend on standby who is no longer standing by but actually sitting in arrives. Now we're on our way to the hospital.

10 P.M.—We arrive at the hospital and are sent to the LDRP (Labor Delivery Recovery and Postpartum) room for monitoring and to make sure "it's time."

10:30 P.M.—It is. More water breaks. Contractions are getting nasty and are five to seven minutes apart.

10:31 P.M.—I politely ask where the epidural man is.

10:45 P.M.—The labor nurse asks me a string of medical history questions, some a bit personal. My only allergy, I reveal, is Dial soap.

10:48 P.M.—I sign for the epidural. I ask—although not quite as politely as I did seventeen minutes earlier—where the epidural man is.

11 P.M.-1:30 A.M.—I spend two-and-a-half hours of hard labor watching the local news, Leno, Arsenio, and Letterman without actually watching them as I use a tissue box, sink drawers,

and plastic glove dispenser as focal points. Bryan goes home to get the battery for our video camera. I testily ask where the epidural man is seven times.

1:32 A.M.—Wearing a large red *E* on his chest and a long flowing cape down his back, Epidural Man arrives!

1:45-3 A.M.—I take a cat nap while listening to *CBS News Overnight* and have a political conversation with the relief labor nurse about Clinton's third choice for attorney general. Bryan sleeps through this exhilarating conversation.

3-3:30 A.M.—I prepare myself to push while watching the Home Shopping Network. By the way, you can get a DiscMan for $139.98.

3:30-4:07 A.M.—PUSH!!!!!

4:09 A.M.—The doctor places Kyle on my chest. Bryan cuts the cord. We bond with our new son until 5:15 A.M. Bryan then calls his parents in South Carolina at 6 A.M. and goes home for some sleep and to relieve my good friend on standby who's there watching Courtney, who sleeps through the whole thing. I, too, use the next hour-and-a-half for sleep.

And, thus, nearly nine months of waiting has ended in the birth of our gorgeous baby boy. Well, I shouldn't say "gorgeous"; he might get a complex. Handsome is much better. He has his daddy's cleft and looks a lot like Courtney.

Like a bride who vaguely remembers walking down the aisle, I vaguely remember all that went on during those seven hours. I remember Carol, the labor nurse, telling me soon after I arrived, "Check your modesty at the door and pick it up after you leave." Would that be a great saying for a refrigerator magnet or what? I remember her successor, the first shift nurse, was named Sally Field. Funny, she didn't look like Gidget. I remember regretting what I had for supper just two hours before labor started: one-and-a-half bowls of macaroni and cheese (or is it cheese and macaroni?), two buttercreams, and one orange slice gumdrop. And I remember that a VBAC is much better than a C-section.

Now I can look forward to losing weight. I'm not sure how I'll do it—maybe by sweatin' to the oldies. Right now I look about six months pregnant, and when I weighed on a scale down the hall, it showed I lost just six pounds. (How did I *gain* a pound in a few hours?)

I'm glad I kept a day-to-day diary since I discovered I was pregnant—or more accurately, since *Bryan* discovered I was pregnant and told me so—because I don't plan on being pregnant again. I mean, this is it.

But happily, I will remember it forever.